MINISTERING TO GAY TEENAGERS

Practical Help for Youth Workers and Families

BY SHAWN HARRISON

YouthMinistry.com/TOGETHER

Ministering to Gay Teenagers
Practical Help for Youth Workers and Families

Copyright © 2014 Shawn Harrison

group.com
simplyyouthministry.com

Credits
Author: Shawn Harrison
Executive Developer: Jason Ostrander
Chief Creative Officer: Joani Schultz
Editor: Rob Cunningham
Copy Editor: Stephanie Martin
Art Director: Veronica Preston
Production Artist: Brian Fuglestad
Production Manager: DeAnne Lear

ISBN 978-1-4707-1358-4

10 9 8 7 6 5 4 3 2 1   20 19 18 17 16 15 14

Printed in the United States of America.

DEDICATION

Dedicated to Emily Harrison, my best friend and true
love. I cannot imagine my life without you.

To everyone who has walked with me during this long
journey, I humbly thank you and appreciate everything. I
am here today because of your love and support.

TABLE OF CONTENTS

PART 1:
THIS JOURNEY

CHAPTER 1:

MY STORY

When I was about 14, I remember watching a news segment that showed two guys kissing each other and thinking to myself, "That's what I am…*gay*." Ever since I could remember, I had liked guys. In my early teen years, I tried dating girls and even tried having sex with girls; but for the most part, those physical things never provided the same satisfaction that my attractions for guys did.

I knew I was different, and the comments of others confirmed it. I didn't flirt with girls, shoot guns, or work on cars. I didn't play or follow sports religiously. I hated gym class. I was an art major who loved the theater, choir, and writing poetry in coffeehouses. As my peers would attest, I was a typical gay teenager. While my small group of friends loved my differences, many of my peers rejected them. "Fag," "Homo," "Queer," "Sissy," "Freak," and other slurs were my nicknames. Some days I wondered if they were my actual name and if "Shawn" was someone different.

The most popular name for me, though, was "Faggot." Sometimes it was a short murmur—"Fag"—and other days it was drawn out with an echo—"F-f-f-a-a-a-a-g-g-g-o-t"—followed by laughter. I wasn't the only gay student in my school; I had other classmates who were gay. However, I was the most vocal of the group. I was proud of who I was, and I desperately wanted people to accept me for who I was. By 12th grade, some began to publicly accept my friends and me, but largely, students in our school couldn't tolerate our existence. And I saw no point in trying to make amends.

My biggest adversaries in school weren't jocks, though they did bully me. The most vocal people against me were Christians. Every day I was damned to hell—and while other "sinners" had a chance at God's love and forgiveness, my friends and I were never offered such hope. This condemnation further sealed my anger and hatred toward God—a being that I'd heard about growing up but didn't know or understand personally. Because people didn't take time to know me or even understand me, they saw me only as a label and not a person. One of my deepest needs as a gay teenager was to be known and liked for who I was.

I was proud to be gay, but I wasn't happy with my life. Though bold on the outside, I was deeply depressed and suicidal inside. No one truly knew the cliff I was standing at—not even my closest friends. I had attempted suicide a couple of times; each time, something (or Someone) stopped me.

DIFFERENT TIME, SAME ISSUE

My story took place in the '90s, and while times have changed, my experience still resembles what many gay[1] teens today face. In fact, with students coming out as early as middle school, life is a lot harder for gay teenagers now than when I was that age. Suicide is on the rise,[2] and the issue of kids being bullied remains significant, especially for gay teenagers.[3] These patterns need to change.

While society is trying to be proactive, it seems that the church spends more time being reactive. However, the body of Christ needs to be at the forefront of proactively loving and ministering to gay teenagers. This needs to be done regardless of their response and regardless of time factors. The church is long overdue in stepping out of its comfort zone and embracing a group of people who need to experience the love of Jesus like never before. And I believe one particular group in the church can bring this game change: youth workers.

This book isn't about proving a theological position on homosexuality, nor is it a book of blame and judgment. The purpose of *Ministering to Gay Teenagers* is to equip youth workers, churches, and families to love gay teenagers where they are, through the means of God's love and identity. While the majority of our conversation will focus on gay teenagers, many of the principles found in this book also are relevant when ministering to gay adults.

Ministry to the gay community isn't as difficult as some people might believe, but it does require time and investment, much like any other ministry requires. The main difference is that ministering to gays and lesbians requires even deeper authenticity in our love, character, truth, and presence, because of the years of mistreatment from the church toward this community. A lack of authenticity in these areas will cause your ministry to crumble. In this standard, then, we must understand and respond in the ways of Jesus.

AN OPPORTUNITY FOR THE CHURCH

The foundation of homosexuality is deep and complex. Whether genetics or family environment plays a sole part in one's homosexuality—the nature vs. nurture debate— or whether it's a mixture of both, the fact remains that gays and lesbians are a part of today's culture and family structure. This book doesn't attempt to resolve or take sides in the debate over the causes of homosexuality. It's my conviction, however, that regardless of the innate structure around homosexuality, the influence of society—positive and negative—plays a large role in how a teenager embodies his or her same-sex attractions.

Within the following chapters, I'll offer my thoughts on the relationship between someone's homosexuality and faith, but I recognize that other Christians may disagree with my conclusions. My intent is simply to spur people toward an honest conversation about homosexuality and about how we respond to people who have a sexual identity that's different from our own. The question is how we will respond. I want to push all of us from theory toward practical action. Some Christians are trying to do this, but now it's time for the greater church to awaken and do the same.

The same grace that was offered to you, as you entered into a relationship with God, must be extended to all who walk through the doors of our churches. The church must not compromise truth, but it must not withhold grace either. This truth is especially vital in a youth ministry. As more teenagers are coming out to family and friends, our youth rooms are often the entry point in which gay students first experience God. How they first encounter God—personally and communally—and how people react to them can determine their subsequent steps.

THE POWER OF AUTHENTIC FRIENDSHIP

I was never a part of a youth group growing up. I walked away from a shallow acquaintanceship with God and decided it was better to be agnostic. If God wasn't for me, I wasn't going to be for him, either. As I said earlier, Christians were my biggest intimidators and condemners—that is, except for one. I became friends with Yvonne in 11th grade. All I knew of her was that she was a Christian and that we belonged to the same SADD (Students Against Destructive Decisions) chapter at school.

After some brief times of hanging out, we soon became good friends. She, my best friend (who was gay), and I quickly became an inseparable trio. My friend and I knew what Yvonne believed, but we also knew she was different from other Christians we'd met. For the first time in my life, I physically saw Jesus Christ within a person.

Yvonne never preached to us, she didn't slam the Bible over our heads—in fact, I don't think she ever read her Bible to us—and she didn't force us to attend church or youth group. My friend and I attended on our own, about two times, but it was because of the friendship we had already established with Yvonne. She really stood by us and our other gay friends because she valued her friendship with us, and we valued our friendship with her.

She was there for us when my best friend and I dated each other, broke up (several times), and had failed relationships with other guys. She heard our doubts about God, and she stood beside us when other Christians condemned us. On the other side, my friends and I saw Yvonne slip up in her walk with Jesus. We saw her ask for forgiveness, we heard her own questions about God, and we stood by her as she tried to stand for her morals.

Whether Yvonne knew it or not, she was planting authentic seeds into my life through her actions and love. God was using her to change my life, though neither of us knew it. On July 14, 1996, a month after I graduated, I chose to follow Jesus Christ as my Savior. Yvonne was the first person I called; she was also the first person to give me a Bible. Later she told me that each time she had picked me up or dropped me off, she had prayed that I would see and follow Christ as my Lord and Savior. Those faithful prayers were heard.

DESIRING MORE OF GOD

In those subsequent days as a young Christian, I decided for myself that I wanted to "change" my identity focus—one that fit my new life as a follower of Christ. I had no idea what I was doing, and though people tried to offer advice and support, I kept struggling to find who I really was. It's not that I had suddenly lost all my attractions toward men—I hadn't. Instead, I began to choose that I was no longer going to allow my attractions toward men to lead my life and define who I was. As I grew closer to Christ—and believe me, this took a long time—I began to experience more freedom in denying my own desires for men, while growing a greater zeal to desire more of God.

As I grew in this newfound freedom, I began to realize and understand that we're all born with certain tendencies—some being useful and some being harmful. In reading the Bible and believing what the

Bible says, I began to comprehend that I was born with a sinful nature, just like everyone else. Because of this, we're all prone to act upon temptations that come our way—such as greed, lying, stealing, adultery, lust—but we also can choose to *not* act upon given temptations.

This is how free will works: God gives us a choice to either do what is right or do what is wrong. My sinful nature caused me to choose my own ways in life, instead of what God wanted—and it still tempts me to make that choice! I was quickly becoming aware that I was in a serious battle, one in which I was a key player and where I was the "ground" being fought over (see Romans 6–8; Galatians 5; and Ephesians 6:10-20).

In this understanding, I felt God was asking me to resist my attraction toward men, to begin to see that acting upon my attractions was sinful, and to follow passionately after him. Again, this was over a four-year period—from age 19 to 23—of growing, wrestling, doubting, trusting, and struggling with everything I was learning and reading about God. Sometimes I walked away during this period, because the journey was asking too much of me. What brought me back each time was God's hounding presence; he wouldn't leave me alone! I had no clue what I was doing. Eventually I grew satisfied in my love for God, and I was fine with whatever God asked of me—as long as I was following him, I knew I would be OK.

By God's awesome grace, I met a woman whom I fell in love with, and we married in May 2001. From the beginning, my wife, Emily, has known about my past and struggles. God has used her in mighty ways, as we have questioned things together and have walked faithfully on the path God has set before us. It's very humbling to be married—at times I really don't feel like I deserve it, nor do I feel like I deserve to be a father of three awesome kids. That's the beauty of God's grace, though: We get what we don't deserve.

I realize my story doesn't speak for everyone's situation, as God calls each of us to our own unique journey with him. I also realize not everyone will agree with me on this, but I don't believe homosexuality is something that people can turn on or off at any given moment, nor can others change someone. In fact, the issue of "change" looks different for everyone, as we'll look at in the following chapters.

But here's the main point we need to keep at the forefront. Jesus came to offer life—abundant, eternal life—where death once reigned. In his death and resurrection, we're transformed into new creations. Through him, we have the power of the Holy Spirit to accomplish what seems impossible, as long as our focus is on him and not ourselves.

The issue isn't whether one deals with same-sex attractions or attains "normal" attractions. It's not even about marrying someone of the opposite sex or staying celibate. The central issue is whether we will forsake everything to follow Christ. And last time I checked, Scripture calls every person to do just this.

CHAPTER 2:

UNDERSTANDING SAME-SEX ATTRACTIONS

"I feel disconnected from God because of my same-sex attractions," Luke[4] shared with me over coffee one day. A teenager attracted to other guys, Luke wants to love God—and wants to eventually get married and become a dad. He wants his same-sex attractions to end, because he believes he can't walk with God faithfully—much less love God—while dealing with these attractions. I'm trying to help Luke process these beliefs and understand that he can love and follow God despite being attracted to guys.

From teenagers like Luke to Christian parents to church leaders, there are misconceptions in the relationship between faith and same-sex attractions. Some argue that no true disciple of Christ could have these types of attractions. I argue that they can, and some mostly definitely do—including me. I firmly believe that one's attractions don't determine one's salvation and sanctification through Jesus Christ. Attractions are just that: attractions. Though they can lead us toward temptation and sin, they are not in and of themselves sin. They don't define a person, nor do they constrain or limit that person.

In fact, I'm at a place where I actually praise God for my same-sex attractions. Nothing has drawn me closer to the love of Jesus Christ than my same-sex attractions. Through them, God has revealed deep truths of who he is and who I am in him, and I've seen the gracious power of my Savior firsthand. I've stopped asking him to take away the very thing that keeps me positioned before his throne.

ADDRESSING THE BASICS

Contrary to a popular belief, especially within evangelical circles,[5] I don't believe a person chooses to have same-sex attractions. Teenagers don't wake up one day saying, "I think I'll be gay today." I never did, and neither did my friends. In fact, people come out usually after months or years of debate with themselves. The process is often long and overwhelming. Therefore, the idea that gay people—especially teens—can just *choose* to be either gay or straight seems ridiculous and even damaging.

The only choice that occurs is when people decide whether to act upon their attractions. Even then, I would say that some people can't help but pursue their attractions, because to them it's what comes naturally. The majority of heterosexuals can't understand this, because they don't understand how someone can like the same sex. To them it's so unnatural. Likewise, many homosexuals don't understand how someone can like the opposite sex, because in their eyes it's unnatural. Both sides speak from their own perspective.

Instead of engaging in debates with megaphones, we need to be willing to walk in the shoes of another person. Speaking to the Christian community, we need to listen more and talk less (James 1:19). Maybe in our listening, we'll begin to understand the complexity gays and lesbians go through. Maybe in our listening, we'll earn the right to speak into their lives God's truth of who he is and who they are.

Saying that gays and lesbians feel their attractions are natural is probably messing with your mind right now, but it's true. For many of them, dating and even marrying someone of the same sex is a natural hope they have. To do otherwise just feels weird. Are they correct in thinking that their attractions are natural? If we were to measure it against what we read in God's creation account, then no, they are not natural. However, before you go "a-ha," I'm pretty sure you consider some other things to be natural that aren't necessarily natural either, according to God's Word.

Our definition of what is natural has been corrupted by the Fall, every one of us. Therefore, what heterosexuals and homosexuals deem as natural isn't necessarily natural to God. That's why we need to seek common ground here. Every person's heart, mind, and intentions have been corrupted by sin. Left up to ourselves, we cannot rightly discern what is right and wrong. If we're honest, we justify ourselves more than we correct ourselves. Only God and his Word have the right to say, "*This* is true, and *this* is false." We need to align ourselves to God's standard and bypass our own. I appreciate A.W. Tozer's thoughts: "Until we have seen ourselves as God sees us, we're not likely to be much disturbed over conditions around us as long as they don't get so far out of hand as to threaten our comfortable way of life. We have learned to live with unholiness and have come to look upon it as the natural and expected thing."[6]

While we cannot scientifically explain why everyone's sexual orientation isn't heterosexual, we can state factually that we live in a world that has fallen from God's original design. And because we live within this reality, all of creation has felt and continues to feel the ramifications of sin's effect. We have been made in the image of God (Genesis 1:26-27), yet the curse of Adam's sin falls upon us (Romans 5:18-19). Everything around us, the Apostle Paul says, awaits God's total restoration of all things, which occurs at the Second Coming of Christ (Romans 8:20-25).

LIVING IN A BROKEN WORLD

It doesn't take a genius to see that our present-day culture isn't Christ-centered. We live in a society that tells us to live by our own standards. We lack a desperate and constant need for God in our lives—at least, this is how the majority of the world lives today. Our culture also loves labels. We love to promote tolerance, but we refuse tolerance to those we disagree with. We protest for love, but our definition of love is so skewed that its truest meaning has been lost. Whether we want to admit it or not, things are broken—seriously broken.

This brokenness within the culture bleeds into the family. Around 26 percent of children (21.8 million) under the age of 21 live in single-parent households.[7] Common issues such as divorce, cohabitation, affairs, addictions, selfishness, and materialism continue to fester within the American church, breaking apart what God has instituted. And too many of us are OK with how the definition of truth has gone from absolute to subjective. In a hard truth to swallow, the book of Judges speaks about where we are currently: *They soon turned aside from the way in which their fathers had walked, who had obeyed the commandments of the Lord, and they did not do so.... Everyone did what was right in his own eyes (Judges 2:17; 17:6).*

I think it can be accurately said that the downward spiral of society and the erosion of Christian values have played a significant part in teens and adults questioning their sexual identity. I'm not pointing my finger at parents in blame for their child being gay or bisexual, nor am I stating that one's environment is the main factor for their sexual orientation. Too many parents hold unwarranted guilt and shame upon themselves for their child's sexuality, which unnecessarily adds to the burden of the journey. However, there's substantial evidence that points to the argument that while one's sexuality is at times complex, certain key factors do play a role in one's identity development. The point is this: Most teens and adults have opposite-sex attractions, while others have same-sex attractions. The focus needs to be on living the life God calls us toward in faithfulness. We must offer a safe place where all people—straight, gay, married, celibate—can build one another up in love, faith, and good works (Hebrews 10:24-25).

GAY CHRISTIANS?

I was at a conference recently where author and counselor Joe Dallas gave a talk on understanding pro-gay theology.[8] He ended the session by talking about gay Christians in general. Dallas shared a challenging statement: We cannot rightly assert that an openly gay person isn't a born-again Christian. Giving examples of the people in the Corinthian church, and Jesus' words to the churches in Revelation, Dallas stated that there are many born-again Christians who live carnal lives. Though their actions don't always adhere to Christ's example, he said, we cannot judge their heart and conversion to Christ.

Just as you and I have things we refuse to hand over to Christ, so others walk in the same manner. I still have much to surrender to Christ, and some things are truly hard to give up, but this doesn't make me a non-believer in Christ. Rather, my faults only affirm that I am still a person in need of an all-powerful Savior who needs to keep refining me from the inside out. Just as Jesus didn't ask the woman to clean up her appearance before she anointed him (John 8:1-11), neither should we expect people to clean themselves up before choosing to follow Jesus as their Savior. Like God our Father, we must follow the example in the parable of the prodigal son and run to embrace those who come home—just as they are and not as they should be (Luke 15:20-24).

In a recent college survey done by the Gay Christian Network (GCN), researchers interviewed about 3,000 students concerning homosexuality. One statistic stuck out above the rest for me. When presented with the statement "It's a sin to be gay, even if you don't have sex," 43.9 percent of evangelical young adults either agreed or strongly agreed.[9] This deeply troubles me. As I stated earlier, I believe a person can be a Christian and have same-sex attractions. Their coming out doesn't negate their Christianity. Although you may disagree with their calling themselves *gay* or referring to themselves as a *gay Christian*, this is a battle not worth fighting. While some gay Christians hold to a biblical view of sexuality and others don't, both feel strongly that the word *gay* needs to be joined to their identity.

My personal conviction is that our only identity should be that of Christ, and I know many other Christians agree with me. However, we cannot force this belief upon gay Christians just to satisfy our expectations. Too often as the church, we struggle with the word *gay* because we suspect that every person who says they're gay is living against the Scriptures. This isn't always the case, though. Just because a person defines himself or herself as gay, or as a gay Christian, doesn't automatically mean that person prescribes to progressive theology or is involved sexually with the same sex. It means they're attracted to their gender, but I believe that person can still hold to the belief that we receive salvation from Christ alone.

COMMON GROUND

The world is filled with two types of people: those who need Jesus and those who need to grow closer to

Jesus. Every person in this world falls into one of these categories, regardless of their race, nationality, sexuality, and religious background. This is common ground. This is where we need to start.

Instead of debating and arguing with people over whether they're truly Christians, what if we started with Jesus and kept him as the end goal? What if we chose to believe people that they profess faith in Christ and helped them to pursue God in a deeper way? What if we allowed the Holy Spirit to convict and transform a person's heart instead of giving ourselves that responsibility?

This doesn't mean we have to allow an "anything goes" mentality within our ministries or churches. Anything we do outside of God's declared standard is sin—period. However, we *can* look beyond the issue in front of us and see the person behind the issue. Jesus was an expert at this, with his apostles later implementing this mindset, and it's a trait we need to rediscover within the church.

The church isn't called to mimic the likeness and attitudes of the world, but of Christ. In and through him, we're to reflect his likeness and attitude to those around us—even people we disagree with and may have a hard time understanding. The posture of ministry is one of compassion. I love how author and pastor Darrin Patrick describes this posture: "When we look, not glance but look, we see the person, not the problem. When we look at the person, we see they matter to God and ought to matter to us. When we look, we see a person to be loved, not a problem to fix. Only when we look can we experience compassion."[10] From this posture is where ministry to gay, lesbian, bisexual, and transgender people begins. No other posture will work but one of compassion, which calls us to stand upon common ground found at the cross of Jesus.

PART 2:
YOUTH WORKERS

CHAPTER 3:

MINISTRY FOUNDATIONS

Ministry to students must be bathed in compassion. We in ministry must not serve only those we naturally gravitate toward or those who are easy to handle. We are called to serve *all* students, because *every* student needs Jesus—just as much as *we* need Jesus. If you're a youth worker, whether you're ready or not, gay students are either in your ministry or will be coming through your doors.

For some youth workers and youth ministries, ministering to gay teens will be easy. For others, this type of ministry will be difficult. However, hear this truth: For such a time as this has God placed this student (or these students) in your care to reach and shepherd. There is a reason why this encounter has happened—or will happen.

Our compassion comes from Jesus, who loved us while we were still sinners (Romans 5:8). In fact, his compassion for others is a foundational thread throughout the Gospels. As people in need stood before him, Christ looked past their issues, their backgrounds, and sometimes even their faith (or lack of), and he spoke to their personhood. Jesus ministered to people right where they were, always showing them value and purpose. As his followers, then, can we do any less?

We find a great little moment in Luke 9, as Jesus and his followers were leaving a village of Samaritans after being rejected by them. John and James approached Jesus and asked him if they should call fire down from heaven to destroy the people who refused them. According to Luke, Jesus turned to these disciples and rebuked them because he had come to save people, not destroy them. I can just imagine Jesus looking at John and James in sheer bewilderment. Had they not been paying attention? How could they have missed the point, especially after hearing the Sermon on the Mount and the new standard for relationships Jesus was calling people to embrace? They totally spoke before thinking— and how many times do we follow suit? How many times do we place our own expectations and limits onto others in the name of Jesus?

Our Savior is after people. He lavishes compassion upon them. He makes himself known to them. When he walked this earth, he traveled from town to town proclaiming the kingdom of God through words and actions (Matthew 4:23). As his ambassadors, therefore, we are to mimic him, regardless of what challenges lie ahead or how frustrated we might feel. Ministry is messy, because people are messy. It seems Jesus loved getting messy, because he loved people as they were. How about you? Jesus said, *"A new commandment I give to you, that you love one another: just as I've loved you, you also are to love one another. By this all people will know that you are my disciples, if you have love for one another" (John 13:34-35).*

How messy are you willing to get?

TRANSFORMING YOUR HEART

God is compassion, just as he is mercy and grace. These aren't just characteristics of God, but part of his being, and they can be part of our being, too, through him. Here's how the Apostle Paul phrased it: *I therefore, a prisoner for the Lord, urge you to walk in a manner worthy of the calling to which you have been called, with all humility and gentleness, with patience, bearing with one another in love, eager to maintain the unity of the Spirit in the bond of peace (Ephesians 4:1-3).*

It's my deep conviction that the greatest people poised to speak influence into the life of a gay teenager are youth workers. Think about it. If you're a youth worker, you have the ability to present yourself in a variety of safe ways and settings. You can openly offer support from a biblical standpoint that teachers in public schools cannot. You can provide encouragement and compassion that many parents are unsure how to give to their child. Having spoken into so many students' lives already as a youth worker, I cannot help but think that if a youth worker had spoken into *my* life as a teenager, I would not have traveled down many of the roads I followed. I believe student ministry is a vital and effective piece to the life of a teenager—especially one who's gay.

What surprises me most, though, is how many student ministries remain unsafe for gay teens. It would be hard to fully eradicate discrimination and bullying from schools—though I strongly believe we must work toward this goal. However, it doesn't make sense why such problems continue in youth ministries! Of all the places where bullying shouldn't happen, it exists within far too many ministries!

Places of ministry must foster the compassion and safety that Jesus offers to all people, from all points of life. Teenagers are at a delicate place when they come to you and declare that they're gay. For many of them, your response determines if they'll stay connected with you, and sometimes if they'll even stay connected to God. This shouldn't cause you to fear the conversation, but rather wake you up to the need for understanding the issue so you know how to respond effectively. Maybe this has already happened to you, or maybe not—but it will.

Although I'm sure many gay students have already heard people say gay sexual relationships are a sin, not everyone has heard about the love and grace of Christ. The church has been quick to point out the *sin* part but rather slow in pointing out the *love of the Father*. If you truly understand this, then you'll begin to move past the cliché of "love the sinner, hate the sin." Gay and lesbian students are more than "sinners." They're people made by the hand of God, first and foremost. We must see what God sees: his creation. Authentic love—love that extends from the Father—looks past people's faults and into their hearts. Yes, Jesus called out sin, but he first went to the root of the matter: the person's need for him. In taking this approach, Jesus was able to effectively deal with the wrong ways people were striving to attain authentic love through other means. He attacked the heart issue, not the person— and we're called to imitate this.

PREPARING YOUR RESPONSE

I suggest that we all go through a process of checking our hearts and minds concerning gay students. The logic behind this principle—"Before you can make disciples, you must first be a disciple"—also applies to this principle: "How you personally relate to gay students will be reflected in what you teach and how you lead students in your ministry." Therefore, it would be wise to sit with God and pray about gay students you currently work with or the ones who may one day walk through your doors. Just as your personal relationship with Christ impacts your ministry and your students, it also will shape your interaction with any gay students. The more you're connected to Christ, the better prepared you'll be to handle the tough questions and situations coming your way—with all students. As youth ministry pioneer Mike Yaconelli once said, "Our relationship with Jesus is our youth ministry."[11] Our messy and authentic relationship with Jesus gives us credibility as youth workers. Christ is our identity, and this is what we pass on to all of our students.

You need to answer questions such as: *How will I respond to the subject of homosexuality? How will I react around gays and lesbians? What about them bothers me? Do I have any fears about them?* As you begin to process these questions, begin to rid yourself of personal expectations and judgments about and for gay students. God's will and timetable must always rise above our own. I strongly advise doing this *before* you have to face this issue directly. Sit in God's presence and ask him to teach you how to respond to gays and lesbians as *he would*. Practically speaking:

Get educated: The more you learn about things, the better. I recommend having a few helpful resources (in addition to this book) in your office to lend out to students and parents.[12]

Seek God's wisdom, truth, and love: This is a complex issue, so without God's guidance we can become lost in misinterpretations, misunderstandings, and assumptions. More than anything, students need God's truth and love imparted to them. The more you seek God's counsel, the greater your impact will be.

Welcome to the journey: Most gay students will expect adults, especially Christians, to bail on them as soon as they come out. Please, don't bail on a student once you've begun this journey with him or her. Too many times, people have started to walk with gay teens but have left them standing alone when the going got tough. Unless you already have someone to take your place (someone the student already knows and trusts), please do all that you can to stay connected to the student. There are no quick fixes or easy shortcuts through this, but I can speak from experience that the road is easier when gay teenagers have trusted companions walking alongside them. If you bail, eventually the student will bail, too—and most likely from everything.

Gather prayer support: Believe me, for gay teenagers, the journey toward Christ comes with spiritual attacks. The enemy wants them to fail, as he wants you to fail, too. Not only will they need prayer support, but you'll need it, too. Gather a trusted group of people around you to be prayer warriors for you and your students (see 1 Thessalonians 5:17).

Offer healthy and transparent relationships: Based on the teenagers I've counseled over the years, as well as my own personal experience, most same-sex attractions involve broken relationships with members of the same sex. Students with these kinds of broken relationships need to find and connect with healthy same-sex friends (another reason why bailing on them will do damage). It can be beneficial to engage adults who have gone through similar struggles the teenager is facing—although this isn't a prerequisite. Whatever the approach, be sure to use great discernment and prayer. Adults who are connected to gay teens must be spiritually mature. Make sure the adults can handle walking alongside a gay teenager.

Offer counseling as a means of help, not a cure: Some students may not need counseling, while others will. But please understand this: Forced counseling *won't work*, no matter how good the counselor is. *If* a student is ready for counseling, suggest some places that you've *already* investigated. If the student isn't ready, *don't push the issue*. Besides helping the student find outside resources, be sure to find resources for parents, too. Family support groups are a big plus in helping parents stay connected with their gay teenager.

WALKING ALONGSIDE STUDENTS

The first person I came out to was my best friend, who also came out to me at the same time. It was the summer after eighth grade, and we both were able to talk about the things we were processing internally, including things we were confused about (*Am I really gay?*) and the things we were struggling with (*What happens next?*). Around the beginning of 10th grade, I told my family. I called my stepmom first, and then I had her tell my dad, because I was deeply afraid of further separating our relationship. Then I told my mom through a letter that I left in her car so she could read it at work. And I never told my stepdad until years later.

Looking back, I realize I should have handled things differently—for their sake and mine. My parents never wanted to discuss my same-sex attractions, much less my relationships, and because of that I always questioned their love and acceptance of me—and I worried what they were thinking about me. I'm sure how I handled telling them had a lot to do with their silence. After all, it's the kind of conversation no one wants to begin, but one that needs to happen.

When counseling teenagers, I advise them to come out to people they can trust. Coming out and saying they have same-sex attractions is a big step to take. It involves mixed emotions, vulnerability, and trust. Therefore, it's important that they can trust the person they're telling. Clearly, I believe it's beneficial if they confide in a youth worker. Unfortunately, I've heard a lot of negative reaction stories from teenagers who came out to their youth pastors (one of the main reasons why I've written this book). A common response from the typical youth worker involves at least one of three things: denial, awkwardness, or silence. Occasionally, a youth worker will go deeper with a student, asking questions to better understand what's going on. That is the best response, in my opinion.

It's OK to *feel* awkward and nervous, as long as you're not *being* awkward and nervous. Let me explain the difference. Not every person is going to take the news well that their student, or child, is questioning their sexuality. Our natural responses to this news can vary. However, as hard as it might be, I suggest we try to contain our responses *inwardly* and not reveal them *publically*. Despite what our natural tendency may be saying, at this critical moment we need to comfort the person. So simply put, freak out at home and not in front of them. Embrace them, thank them for being honest, and be a comforting support to them.

When a student says, "I'm gay," it's fair to ask them to define what they mean: *Are you just attracted to your gender, or are you looking to date someone?* Allowing the teenager to define the word saves you (and him or her) from the embarrassment of being wrong. Not every gay teen is looking to hook up with someone relationally or physically. In some cases, when teens come out, they're simply looking for a safe place to be themselves as they discover who it is they are. In a way, they're testing the waters.

In the moments following their coming out, you'll want to affirm a few things: God's love for them, your love for them, and your support in whatever form it's needed. Additionally, focus on the main issue, namely their relationship with Christ. If the student isn't a follower of Jesus, then your main concern is that they make the decision to place their trust in Jesus—not so they can become "good heterosexuals," but because of God's great love and sacrifice for them. You want them to take hold of the new life Christ offers for their present dead life. It's important as youth workers and shepherds that we don't impose our personal expectations and biases onto students and adults who are coming to Christ with same-sex attractions.

If the student is already a Christian, then your main concern is growing them closer to Christ. Your objective is shepherding them toward being a disciple of Jesus Christ. Their attractions don't disqualify this person from following Christ, nor do they have to hinder him or her from being a disciple of Christ. The most important foundation you can begin working with them on is their identity in Christ. It's my conviction that everything in our lives centers on this truth. Teenagers—gay and straight—need to build a life around their identity in Christ.

OFFERING WISDOM TO A TEENAGER

Another thing you'll want to discuss with your student is if they've come out to their family. Chances are they have not, though some might have already done this. A big caution: Your job isn't to "out" them or force them to tell their parents about their sexuality. Coming out to one's parents is a very personal and scary situation. Some estimate that 26 percent of gay teenagers are kicked out of the house by their parents for coming out to them. I've talked with many parents who have expressed deep pain and confusion over their child being gay, especially those coming from Christian households. This news isn't something that parents take lightly.

So if the student hasn't come out to his or her parents, I suggest the following process. These are specific suggestions I give teenagers if we're talking face to face:

Take someone with you. Bring along a friend who you've already confided in about your sexuality. I didn't have anyone with me when I told my parents, and I wish I would have. When I called my stepmom, I was so scared to speak that I babbled about nothing for over an hour, until finally I spoke up— not because I was ready but because my nerves were shot. If I'd had someone there with me, I'm sure I would have been able to express myself more clearly and strongly. Another benefit to taking someone with you is that the person can stand up and speak for you if your parents are about to explode in anger or confusion. The person with you can help settle a fight—if one should arise—and calm any tensions by speaking on behalf of both groups.

Tell your parents face to face—not through a letter. This may be one of the hardest parts about coming out to your parents, but it's also the best thing you can do when having this type of talk with them. Talking face to face shows people a few things: You respect them, you've thought through what you're telling them, and you're willing to have an honest conversation about the subject. Face-to-face conversations allow both parties to see (and hear) what the other person is saying—and not saying. A letter is too impersonal for this kind of issue. The person reading it can't see your face or hear your tone, let alone understand the emotion you're going through at this moment. And you won't be able to see the other person's expressions or emotions either, which can be nerve-racking, too.

Be ready to not get the reaction you're hoping for. Please understand that by the time you tell your parents you're gay, you've been processing everything for a long time. You know what's going on, you've accepted who you are, and you're ready for others to fully embrace you, too. Your parents, however, haven't had all this time to process things. Therefore, you really can't expect them to jump up and embrace you as if nothing has changed.

For your parents, everything has changed. And in most cases, accepting change about one's kids is hard to do. Give them room to process through their own questions. They may get really quiet. They may walk out of the room. They may cry. And they may hug and kiss you, telling you that everything is going to be fine. However they respond, let them be, and understand that no matter what, they still love you—you're still their child!

I thought my parents hated me because they didn't talk to me about things. Whenever I tried to bring the subject up, it was ignored. However, looking back, this wasn't the case; they just didn't know how to deal with things. They were confused, hurt, and afraid for me. Yeah, they should have said something, but they just didn't know what to say. What I've learned is that silence isn't always a bad thing. Talk to your parents and allow them time to filter through everything. It's going to take time, for you *and* them, and that's OK. This isn't an issue that one can easily get through—it's going to be a journey for both you and your parents.

In addition to all that advice, I would also suggest the teenager *not* have this important conversation in a public space. Apart from your office, their home, or another close relative's home, this type of conversation isn't appropriate for public environments (such as a restaurant). While the student may feel comfortable out in public, the parents may not. Plus, if the situation does get out of hand, things can be contained more effectively in a personal environment. Though you're a support for the student, you're also a support to the parents hearing this news for the first time. It's a tense position to be in, no doubt, but a position that I believe Christ calls us to fill.

SUPPORTING THE PARENTS

As I said previously, when gathering information for yourself concerning homosexuality, make sure you gather things for parents, too. Most likely, Mom and Dad (or stepparents, guardians, or grandparents, depending on the teenager's family situation) have no clue where to find help and support, so be the person who offers them trusted resources.

If you're meeting with a family whose child is about to come out as gay, here are some pointers for navigating the conversation.

1. **During the conversation you'll fill three roles:** a support, a "referee" if things get heated, and a prayer warrior.

2. **Help the parents hear what their child is saying to them, and what the child isn't**

saying. This may take a while, but allow the teenager to get everything out in the open.

3. **Help the parents respond in a way that doesn't demean or "wall up" their child.** This isn't a time for them to yell, get angry, pass judgment, or belittle the situation. Their response should be one of love and support.

4. **If there are siblings in the house, and they're old enough to participate in this conversation, bring them in to discuss what they're feeling.** Allow them to express themselves, as they're most often overlooked in times like this. *If the parents object, don't force sibling involvement.*

5. **When all is said and done, offer your commitment to help in any way you can.** Speak in "we" sentiments, letting them know you're with them all the way.

6. **Finally, before leaving, offer to pray with everyone.** If they don't want to pray, do so in your car on the way home. A big reason I'm where I am today is because people never stopped praying for me.

Be ready if the topic of sex turns up when talking to parents and their child. In most cases, the mom or dad will bring up the topic, and they'll do so out of fear for their child. Remind them that not every gay teenager is looking to engage in sexual activity. In fact, many gay teens are afraid to act upon their attractions because they don't know what will happen. *(I have some friends who have never acted upon their attractions at all!)* So calm the parental fears, but also offer realistic help and hope if sexual issues have arisen.

If the teen is viewing any kind of pornography—gay or straight—parents should help their child break free from this behavior. Many gay teenagers will begin looking at straight porn and then eventually move to gay porn. More often than not, the viewing of such content ties into and fuels their same-sex attractions. Help the parents set up accountability with their child on all computers and mobile devices.[13]

My hope and prayer is that after things settle down, parents will accept your offer for continued support and guidance. Here's some advice on walking alongside parents of gay children—you may need to repeat some things often to parents, and maybe even to yourself.

Remember that God remains lovingly sovereign. Throughout Scripture, God assures us that he will never leave us or forsake us. You can hold tight to this promise, and you can help parents do the same. Though you don't have all the answers, God does. Rest in the assurance of who God is and what he promises.

Be compassionate. Help create a safe space for parents to ask honest questions about their situation, and allow them to freely express themselves. Some might yell, cry, use crude language, bring up difficult doubts, or just sit in silence. The goal is to help them express themselves freely in a safe place. Assure parents that no matter what, you'll be there to walk alongside them. Additionally, assure them of God's love and promises through Scripture, especially the truth that he will never leave us or forsake us.

Don't try to answer difficult questions. You won't have all the answers, and neither will parents. Some questions may never be answered, while others won't be answered the way we want them to be. Help parents seek God in the midst of their uncertainty and cling to the firm promises of Scripture. (Notice a pattern here?)

Surrender expectations. Pastor and author Tim Geiger notes that "neither you nor the parents can convince the child that he or she is wrong. Only the Lord can ultimately do that. What will generally make the biggest difference in the life of a child is parents who model the faithful, yet uncompromising love of God... Praying for change in their child's life is appropriate. But it may not happen immediately—or ever."[14] In this issue of change, assure the parents that while God *does* transform those who seek him, his ways aren't ours and his idea of a "healthy identity" transcends our own understanding.

Keep connected to God. It's natural for parents to ask God, "Why," and we need to give them room to do so. But also help them ask God, "How do we help our child?" Encourage parents to keep pressing into God, even in his silence. Help parents focus on their own relationship with Christ, especially through honest prayer with each other and through reading Scripture.

Ask about the future. Again, Geiger notes, "When the storm clears, ask the parents how they could re-establish a sense of normalcy in their lives and in their relationship with their child."[15] Strive to go beyond the "I want my child to change now" discussion. Remind parents that even though their child has same-sex attractions, their future hasn't been forsaken. Though things are different from what they had hoped for, God can and will use their child for great things.

Pray with and for parents. This may sound like a no-brainer, but it's essential to take time to pray. The parents need your in-person prayers, and they need you praying in the days, weeks, and months ahead, as they continue walking this road.

Encourage them to bring others into their journey.
Whether it's a support group or even a weekly prayer group consisting of friends, help the parents connect with others who can be trusted and committed in walking with them through this journey. This new journey will challenge the faith of the parents—as well as the child. Giving them a strong, supportive Christian presence is vital. Geiger says parents need to "hold on to the biblical position on same-sex relationships in the face of what may be strong, deeply emotional pleas from their child to affirm their lifestyle. This is a painful and difficult place for a parent today. It isn't altogether wrong for parents to want to see their adult son or daughter prospering and being happy…yet, the one thing that will remain painful and grievous is their unwillingness to affirm a lifestyle direction that is contrary to God's design in Scripture."[16]

Parents aren't wrong or hateful for not affirming the life their gay child is living. However, what is important, and where the local church needs to support parents the most, is that the parent loves their child—*unconditionally*—and that they hold to God's truth—*unashamedly*. Affirming a behavior that goes against the Word of God isn't showing that person love—especially the love of God. Affirming a person, while holding to biblical truth, *does* show the love of God to others, even to those who refuse to listen. Standing for the truth is hard, but Jesus has called us to do just that (through the guidance of the Holy Spirit). Parents don't need to *hear* Bible verses as much as they need to *see* them being lived out. Make a commitment to stand beside parents of gay children, no matter what. Additionally, make a commitment to personally love and support their gay child, no matter what.

A WORD ABOUT CHANGE

I hate the phrase "pray away the gay." The journey I'm on isn't so simplistic. I am a contender in a daily battle to keep my eyes, mind, and heart fixed on Jesus Christ, the founder and perfecter of my faith (Hebrews 12:1-2). Each day is a new decision to offer myself as a living sacrifice; each day is a new decision to either live out of my own strength or his (Romans 12:1-2; 2 Corinthians 12:9-10). This journey isn't about just praying away something I don't want; it's about pursuing Someone who's greater than myself.

The period from July 1996, when I became a Christian, to mid-August 2000 was a huge time of struggle for me. One of my biggest hang-ups was that I wasn't *changing*. After years of trying to change, I still felt attractions toward guys. I was convinced I'd never experience change, concluding that God either was punishing me or hated me. For years, I literally prayed for God to either give me straight lusts or to take away my sexual drive completely. (Wrong type of prayers, I know.) However, what I've learned from those years is that when we define heterosexuality or marriage as the goals of change, we've missed the point, and we allow others who are gay to miss the point as well.

Yes, marriage is a great thing, and I hope many people who deal with same-sex attractions can experience it (with the opposite sex), but marriage doesn't make you a "man" or a "woman." We, the church, must take this expectation and burden off our gay brothers and sisters, especially those who truly have no desire to date or marry the opposite sex. There are those who are able to leave their same-sex attractions totally behind and marry. Others are able to deal with their attractions, and not succumb to them, and either get married or live a life of celibacy. We must celebrate those seeking marriage or celibacy, and support both journeys in the community life of the congregation.

Everyone who encounters Christ experiences change (2 Corinthians 5:17). Made anew in Christ, our identity changes from "me" to "him." To be changed by Christ means we start embracing the Father's unconditional love, instead of clinging to the lies about our worthlessness. It involves taking hold of God's promises and claiming them as our own. Our Christian journey is about being disciples who live in the identity as God's child, and who walk in his power and for his glory. This faith is about being people who are captured by God's wild and passionate love, and who are satisfied in all that Christ is and offers. When it comes to the topic of change for gay teens and adults, this is the only change we uphold.

In the next two chapters, I want to unpack three core values essential to ministering to gay teenagers: *belong, believe,* and *be transformed.* Each builds upon the other; each centers on our identity in Christ.

CHAPTER 4:
CORE VALUE OF "BELONG"

The struggle with self-hatred engulfed me for years. More days than not, I wanted to die. I hated everything about myself, including seeing my sexuality as a flaw with everything else.

I had a love/hate emotion toward my sexuality: I hated not feeling "normal," but I loved the community being gay offered. My friendship circle was tight. I could call these friends at any time, knowing their shoulders and ears were always mine if I needed. And there was a support group for gay teens and young adults that my friend's mom used to take us to on Friday nights. It was led by a gay pastor of a local church, and the living room was always filled with people, like me, who were looking for a place to fit in and be themselves.

Looking back on this memory, I guess you could say this was the first youth group I attended. The pastor would tell us how much his God loved us, and that while the world was mean, there was safety in our community. I didn't buy into the God talk, but I did love feeling safe at the group. Looking back, I can see that God was planting seeds within me.

After becoming a Christian, I started attending a church with a friend who took me under his wing. About a year later, I had a falling out with my faith and left everything for a few months. Coming back, I realized the wrong I did and the hurt I caused, especially to my friend. I showed up at his house to seek forgiveness but left unforgiven and deeply wounded. He told me that my falling out was unchristian of me, and that he could no longer be my friend. It was a mistake to even get this close to you, he said.

I left the church, and I almost left my faith completely. I reckoned that church wasn't a safe place to talk about my homosexuality. Even though I was now a Christian, I would be accepted only if I never brought up my unacceptable past—at least that's what I told myself.

At the next church I attended, I met with the pastor and told him some of my story, but still protected myself by not telling him everything. In fact, I never shared my full testimony with another person in the church during the entire 4½ years I attended. A guy from my high school was a member of this church, and through God's working he remains my best friend today. While Pete knew about me in high school, he never asked about this part of my past, and I didn't offer up anything.

During those years at my church, God began revealing deep truths from Scripture, and I truly began growing a lot. I loved my church family, and I knew they loved me. However, the issue I really needed to be talking about was something that I felt I couldn't, based on my previous church experience. Looking back, I wish I would've taken a chance and opened myself up to them. I'm sure I could've saved myself from a lot of unpleasant experiences that set me back further in my faith journey. I stayed silent because to me, it was easier to struggle silently than to lose everything that was important to me.

I wouldn't begin talking about my full testimony until 2006, a decade after beginning to follow Christ. I didn't trust the church to be a safe place, even though people showed me love. My stories resemble numerous other gay people's stories, from being paralyzed by self-hatred to desperately wanting to be known by their Christian community. To them, churches and even youth ministries were not and are not safe places to belong. That's why I'm so passionate about making sure gays and lesbians encounter the power of belonging from the body of Christ—that's what they need, period. I'm deeply committed to ending the awkwardness between people who are gay and people who are the church, by proclaiming the transforming power of Christ's identity, which joins us together.

THE POWER OF BELONGING

Identity is an essential part of our core as humans. We all wonder *"Who am I?"* and *"Why am I here?"* and we go through life trying to answer these questions ourselves, only to keep drinking from self-made cisterns that hold no living water (Jeremiah 2:13). I'm convinced that apart from Christ, these questions will remain unanswered within every person. We find our core identity in Christ alone, and it's from this identity that we truly begin to live as freed people. Here's what the Apostle John wrote: *See what kind of love **the Father has given to us,** that we should be called **children of God; and so we are.** The reason why the world doesn't know us is that it did not know him. **Beloved, we are God's children now,** and what we will be has not yet appeared; but we know that when he appears we shall be like him, because we shall see him as he is. And **everyone** who thus hopes in him purifies himself as he is pure (1 John 3:1-3, emphases added).*

I remember reading this passage for the first time in a devotional. I was at a place where I was tired of looking for quick fixes from God. I was ready to be satisfied with who he was and who I was in him. When I read

John's words at that moment, everything began to click. Through them, God began speaking to my walled-up and wounded heart: *I chose you to be my child, transformation is connected to your faith and trust in me, and from this point forward, Christ is your central focus*. Through these words, God began breaking the bondage of my deep-rooted self-hate. I began to believe that I was meant for something more, solely because the God of the universe called me his child. These words have also shaped the way I serve students, adults, and families with gay children.

Millions of people need to hear and embrace these same truths, especially the students you encounter within your ministry and community. People need to know who they are, what their purpose is, and how both of those answers can be found in Christ alone. For too long, the church has held the mentality that people must first clean up and adhere to our beliefs before we can accept them—before God can accept them. Not only is this bad theology, but it's also a damaging yoke placed upon people. The good news of Jesus teaches truth that is quite different: Because we belong to God, we can believe in him and experience transformation by the presence and power of his Spirit. Our faith and our transformation are rooted in our identity as children of God.

While I was still a sinner, Christ died for me. How great was God's love for me, that while I was still pursuing gay relationships, God was pursuing me with a deep, unconditional love. This love draws all of us to God and is the same love God desires to shine through us in reaching out to others. Gay students need to not only hear about this love but also see this love from those who call themselves Christians. These teenagers need to know that they're made in the image of God, and that they belong to him and to our student ministries. By encountering God's radical love, teenagers can begin to discover their value and worth through God's eyes, and I believe this will help them see that what God offers is greater than what the world offers.

I think this is why the disciples gave up everything to follow Jesus as fast as they did. Being fishermen, they seemed content with their work and lifestyle. However, I'm sure deep inside they wanted more out of life, possibly hoping for a second chance. In the middle of their workday, Jesus approached James, John, Simon, and Andrew. Without asking for their credentials, he spoke a simple phrase: "Follow me." In those two words, Jesus spoke a new identity over them, filled with deep value and worth. They followed Jesus because he chose them, and they continued following him because they were secure in their identity. A Jesus-centered identity is the fuel his disciples need in their mission to the world. As my friend Chris McAlister teaches, "Being secure in our identity brings clarity to our mission, which allows us to build healthy community."[17] This is the power of belonging, which is the first core value of a student ministry where gay teens feel accepted and safe.

THE YOUTH ROOM

What environment should our youth rooms have? What boundaries should be set in place? How do we make everyone feel safe and welcomed in our youth groups? To answer these questions, I want to offer some ideas we've implemented into every student ministry I've led.

At the beginning of the new school year, I hand out a Student Ministry Covenant[18] that every student must sign, along with his or her parent. I'm often heard telling our youth, "If you're gonna tell people you're a Christian, then you'd better live like a Christian," which is why I have them sign the covenant. Within this covenant, I explain the expectations I have for every student in our ministry. Beyond asking students to respect the property of our church and other places, I call students to respect others and themselves, and above all to honor Christ. Some of these things are no-brainers, but I've learned that things need to be repeated often. Besides, some students really have no clue how to respectfully treat others, much less themselves, because their home environment teaches them differently.

Our students understand that I won't tolerate bullying—of any kind. Offenders will be sent home, on the spot, and will be allowed back only after apologizing to the person and the entire group. I take bullying very seriously, and all youth workers ought to do likewise, especially if gay students are involved. School environments are largely plagued with bullying, which gay students face on a day-to-day basis. That environment shouldn't carry into the youth room. I strongly believe our ministries should influence our schools with the constant presence of Christ in our students' actions and attitudes.

In our youth ministry, I've outlawed gay jokes and imitations—along with other disrespectful stereotypes of people. As I mentioned earlier, my peers in school regularly called me "faggot," including people who claimed to be Christians. That's why I've banned this "f" word from conversations within the youth room. To me, *this* word is more disgusting than *the other* "f" word. I've also banned words like *homo*, *lesbo*, and *dyke*. All of these words place false identity labels upon teenagers, whether they're gay or not. Strive to implement the words of Ephesians 4:29 in your life—to always build up and never tear down.

Regarding PDA, couples aren't allowed to "be all over each other." While we can't stop teenagers from dating, we can ask them to refrain from certain behaviors while at youth services, events, and trips. Setting this standard in advance for *all* students helps to implement this for openly gay teens who show up at youth group. I believe all youth ministries need to proactively establish a PDA boundary, and not wait until it becomes an issue. When an openly gay teen and their boyfriend/girlfriend comes into your ministry, and they want to display their affection, you'll want to be able to point to a boundary already set in place, not one that's made up on the spot just for them. Otherwise, they can rightly call foul on your judgment.

It isn't imperative that you notify students and parents that you have a gay teen in your ministry. Outing them in this manner will repel them from your ministry—and maybe even from Christ—faster than anything else. Ask the student if you can share their news with trusted adult volunteers (it's important they can be trusted). Inform the student that you want to share this info in order to help protect them if anything should come about during an event, such as teasing, rumors, and accusations. It would also be beneficial to inform your senior pastor about the situation. This way, if or when parents call or schedule a meeting with you, your senior pastor will be aware and prepared. For more on dealing with specific situations, see Chapter 6, which includes youth ministry FAQs, and Chapter 10, which includes FAQs for churches and church leaders to consider.

I realize we don't live in an ideal world. Things are going to happen if we're around and even if we're not around. However, that shouldn't discourage us from establishing boundaries and expectations in our ministries. While students may not take to heart every lesson taught, I strongly believe that when we in youth ministry integrate the core values outlined here—*belong*, *believe*, and *be transformed*—into everything we teach, students will begin to live out these values beyond the youth room walls. We should aim for at least this response.

PRACTICAL BELONGING

Here are things I share with students on a regular basis, whether during midweek youth services or when we're chatting in a coffee shop.

> **"You have a name."** Our parents give each of us a name at birth. Our name speaks who we are. Similarly, when we follow Jesus, God calls us by names that define who we are. Because gay students often hear profane adjectives describing them all day, many of them forget or dismiss how God refers to them. Christians are sons and daughters of the King, no matter what sin tempts or entraps us. A student's sexuality doesn't define how God sees them; therefore, don't let their sexuality define how they see themselves (see Romans 8:13-17; 1 Peter 2:9-10; 1 John 3:1-3).

> **"You are valued."** Students need to understand that even if family and friends have rejected them, God unconditionally loves them. Just as importantly, he finds great value in them, as evidenced in Jesus' willingness to die for them. Without hesitation, Jesus died for all, knowing that many would reject him. The love God has for each of us existed before the foundations of the world. All teenagers are deeply valuable to God (see Isaiah 43:1-7; John 3:16-17; Ephesians 1:4-8).

"Your life has purpose." With the volume of scars, abuse, and other negative things piling up against them, many students are convinced that there's no hope for a better life, and many chuck their faith in God to the curb. However, God desires to speak his truth over them so they can embrace the essence of his eternal love. Their life isn't over because they have same-sex attractions, and neither is their faith. God isn't looking for perfection from us; rather, he's looking for faith and trust in the One who can do the impossible: himself. We are his workmanship, created for his mission and purpose (see Isaiah 40:21-31; Jeremiah 29:11-14; Ephesians 2:8-10).

"Your past is the past." Just as sexuality doesn't define us, neither do our past actions or temptations. What we struggle with doesn't define who we are or who we will become. In Christ, we're new creations. Many who walk away from unwanted same-sex attractions are fearful that their past will constantly define their present or future. That isn't the case! We can have victory over temptations; we're more than conquerors through Christ! Students need to embrace this reality over the lies of the enemy (see Romans 8:1-2, 37; 1 Corinthians 6:11; 2 Corinthians 3:17; 5:14-17).

Regardless of where students are in their walk with Christ, these things remain true. God's unconditional love for us is greater than the sins we have committed (and will commit). I believe Jesus paints a picture of God in the Gospels as a Father who waits for his children to return and who never stops seeking after his children. I don't believe God sits on some remote cloud waiting to smite us for our continual evil deeds. Yes, in the end God will act in justice toward evil, but in this time, his loving kindness leads us to repentance (Romans 2:4). Some students in your ministry will want to pursue their gay attractions—not necessarily engage in sex but possibly date another gay teenager. Meet them where they are, and remind them of the above truths every chance you get.

For those who want to act upon their gay attractions, assure them of your commitment to walk beside them. Additionally, God still loves them and waits for them to respond back (Luke 15:20). God's love won't stop just because they pursue a relationship with a member of the same sex, just as God's love doesn't stop for other people who follow other paths that might not please him. God reveals that he is compassionate, full of mercy, and abounding in grace (Psalm 145:8)—but he also says we shouldn't test him (Matthew 4:7). God's fullness isn't attained until we're fully pursuing him over ourselves (refer to John 4:7-30 and John 8:1-11).

While I strongly adhere to not giving our students false hope, let us never withhold the hope of the gospel either. What do I mean? Don't tell a gay teen, "You'll get over this someday. Just keep trying harder. If you just do _____, things will get better." This is false hope. Instead, remind teenagers that through Christ all things are possible, that his grace is sufficient for them, that his power is made perfect in their weakness, and that we need God's strength and power in our lives (see Philippians 4:13; 2 Corinthians 12:9-10; Colossians 1:29). This is the hope of the gospel we proclaim boldly.

How we live within the reality of these truths determines how much or how little we see God's power displayed in our lives. We must believe that God is faithful, that God's Word is relevant and sufficient, and that God's power is limitless. However, we must also let God be God and pursue his will, rather than play God and set our own expectations upon our students. As we walk in faith with Jesus, our students will follow alongside.

CHAPTER 5:

CORE VALUES OF "BELIEVE" AND "BE TRANSFORMED"

In the previous chapter, we talked about establishing a core value of "belong" within your student ministry. In this chapter, we'll examine the core values of "believe" and "be transformed." All three values build on each other, laying a framework in which to minister to gay teenagers in your ministry and community. The more we believe in God's Word (Jesus himself), the more God's Word transforms us. Our belief and transformation become apparent to us as we experience the process described in Romans 12:1-2, where Paul calls upon Christians to renew their minds—both new and seasoned believers.

As we help gay teenagers embrace their identity in Christ, we also begin to help them embrace the other truths of Scripture—namely, the promises and challenges of God. However, in doing this, please know that some of our minds need to be renewed as well, especially in terms of how we live out (or fail to live out) the promises and challenges of God ourselves. One such passage is Ephesians 5:1-2—*Therefore be imitators of God, as beloved children. And walk in love, as Christ loved us and gave himself up for us, a fragrant offering and sacrifice to God.*

Because we're God's children, we're called to live lives that imitate his character. Because Christ loved us and died for us, we're called to walk in the same manner of love toward others. Our identity fuels everything about our lives—our mission, our passion, our dreams, and so on. Without a secure identity, we're left to believe anything and everything about life and ourselves. Too many of our students live within this reality day after day. Too many teenagers turn into adults who are willing to wear every other label but the one Christ desires them to put on. This is true for those outside the church and those within the church walls. We need to be people with renewed minds and lives.

AGGRESSIVE LOVE

As Christians, we're very good at doing things for God: five steps to this, practice these routines, say this prayer, wear this and don't do that, and so on. The mindset is simple but flawed: The more we do for God, the better Christians we are, and the better we feel about ourselves. While we may not admit it, we're essentially trying to earn God's love and our place in heaven.

This teaching filters down to teenagers, leaving large numbers of young people abandoning their faith because they can't live up to God's expectations—at least, what they *think* are God's expectations. We need to switch things around, to where we're leading teenagers to live from a place of *being* and not from a place of *doing*. This is key in allowing the Spirit to renew our minds. We don't live through our own self-righteousness but through the righteousness of Christ. "The key to the Christian life is to live out of the reality of who we are so that we can do what God has revealed in Scripture," Darrin Patrick writes.[19]

Jesus is about heart transformation, not just behavior modification. If we simply focus on behaviors, we reduce a relationship with Christ to a list of do's and don'ts, causing us to seriously miss the point. Jesus didn't come to make us good people; he came to bring dead people back to life. In him, we're washed, we're sanctified, we're justified by the Spirit of God (1 Corinthians 6:11). Apart from Jesus is death, but in him is life. This is what our message must be to those around us—teens, adults, straight, and gay. Just as Jesus makes no distinction about who can come to him and receive such life and identity, neither should the church. To make such distinctions causes us to be the "bigger sinner."

As the church, we're so quick to call out homosexuality as the sin above all sins, while ignoring our own faults. This hypocrisy must stop! Don't we realize we're turning people away from God because of our discomfort and ignorance? Don't we realize we stand in greater judgment for turning people away from God because of our careless actions and words? How long will we continue to ignore the words Jesus and the New Testament writers declared about favoritism, loving our enemies, practicing hospitality, and being doers of the Word? Please understand that when gay, lesbian, bisexual, and transgender teenagers come through the doors of any church, they're processing all of those things through their minds. I know this because I was one of them—first as a non-Christian and then as a follower of Jesus—with the same things spinning through my mind.

Going further in Romans 12, Paul talks about *practicing hospitality* (v. 13). This phrase goes far beyond serving cookies, greeting new people, or creating a high-tech, fast-paced experience in a church setting. Looking into the Greek, *practicing* means *to aggressively chase, pursue with all haste,*[20] and *hospitality* means *to love strangers.*[21] Essentially, Paul tells us in Romans 12:13 that being a Christian involves aggressively loving strangers.

So how are we doing on this? As youth workers, are we willing to aggressively love gay teenagers, no matter the cost, no matter the journey, and no matter the outcome?

As I mentioned before, no quick fixes are available; this journey requires intentional time, and it's going to require our comfort levels being stretched wide. Gay teenagers aren't going to believe in Jesus just because you tell them to. They're going to believe in him after they experience him for themselves, and a huge way God does this is through willing people like you and me.

PRACTICAL BELIEVING

While in college, I had two professors who deeply influenced my walk with Christ and my call to ministry. Dr. Wes Gerig, my professor of theology, taught me to trust the Bible as believable and relevant for today. He consistently challenged me to discover this for myself instead of just taking his word. Dr. Wes's basic challenge was this: Here is what we believe as Christians, here are supporting Scriptures from the Bible, now dive in and see if you come to the same conclusions. From him I developed a deep love for the Bible and a deep conviction to desire God's truth over my own. While deeply secure in his own faith, Dr. Wes didn't want his students to just blindly adopt his faith, but to develop their own faith through the truths of God's Word.

Dr. Dave Biberstein, my professor of pastoral ministries, took what Dr. Wes taught and challenged me to read Scripture through a personal and practical lens. His aim was twofold: Apply God's ancient truths to your life today, and live out these truths through God's character. Dr. Biberstein consistently challenged me to be authentic in my faith and teaching, noting that because ministry sometimes is messy, I needed to get messy with others—without fear. Since then, I've taught the same principles to students and adults.

A.W. Tozer writes, "What comes into our minds when we think about God is the most important thing about us."[22] How true this statement is, both for those we lead and for ourselves. Helping teenagers embrace the truth of who they are God and who they are in Christ is a huge foundational piece. The other huge piece, then, is helping students to embrace all of Scripture as God's truth, and connecting their lives to these truths.

Here are some examples of what I mean. If we believe that God is unchangeable and that Jesus is the same yesterday, today, and forever, then what God has spoken in the Bible, he speaks now. If we believe that Jesus is God, then he has spoken not just the red letters but the black letters, too. If we believe that the promises of God apply to us, then the challenges, commands, and even the warnings of God apply to us, too. We cannot take the parts of the Bible we like, the parts we find easy and unthreatening, and disregard the rest as being irrelevant for today. Either we take all of who God is and what God says, or we take none of it. This applies to those who are conservative and those who are liberal within every denomination—and this goes far beyond the topic of homosexuality.

Our job as youth workers isn't to beat God's truth into the minds of our students, but to help them discover God's truth for themselves. In doing this, we help them form their lives around the life God calls us all to, more than the life our world holds up as ideal. One way I help students implement this is by teaching them to find themselves within the Scriptures. They do this by seeking out their identity in the Bible and applying the promises and challenges of God to their present-day life.

We find Paul teaching us this same pattern within every letter he wrote, Chris McAlister notes. "Whether he does it in a single sentence or half the book, [Paul's] usual pattern is to first frame who we are in relation to God.... We work against the pattern God uses when we tell people what to do before they know who they are."[23] Take Ephesians, for example: Chapters 1–3 outline who God is and who we are, and chapters 4–6 examine our call to mission and relationships.

Let me use Romans 8 as another example of what I'm talking about. In counseling gay teens, I give them Romans 8 and ask them to find themselves within the chapter. Here are 22 things Paul says about followers of Christ in Romans 8:

- No condemnation
- Free
- Set apart
- Indwelt with the Spirit
- Life in peace
- Redeemed
- Belonging to Christ
- Children of God
- Heirs of God
- Receivers of a great reward
- Receivers of a great helper
- Receivers of a great hope
- Image of Christ
- Called
- Justified
- Glorified
- Defended by God
- Serving a risen Christ
- Precious to God
- Unconditionally loved
- More than a conqueror
- Joined together in God's story

These things remain true not because of who we are but because of who God is. We can trust what God says, about himself and us, because he remains faithful, even when we're faithless. Pastor and author Neil Anderson shares some wise words we need to help teenagers take to heart: "The major strategy of Satan is to distort the character of God and the truth of who we're. He can't change God and he can't do anything to change our identity and position in Christ. If, however, he can get us to believe a lie, we will live as though our identity [and position] in Christ isn't true."[24] The renewal of our minds is going to take time—a lifetime, actually, thrusting us into a journey with God that is often unpredictable. Our belief in God involves deep trust in God. And one major vessel God uses to develop this faith and trust is authentic community. In other words, transformation happens within community.

PRACTICAL TRANSFORMATION

Just as God is communal (the Trinity), so he has made us to be communal. As our Christian life is about conforming to God's image, so our holiness is about being relationship-focused—with God and others. Going back to Romans 12, for example, Paul says that in light of God's mercies that he had just discussed, we're called to live a life that reflects God's mercy within the means of authentic community. This concept weaves throughout Scripture (see Leviticus 19:11-18; Matthew 5–7; Ephesians 4–6 for discussions on unity and interactions with other people). When God said in Genesis 2 that it wasn't good for man to be alone, I don't believe he was just talking about marriage. Just as the Trinity is firmly united, so Christians are to unite in community, because people left alone are in danger of falling away (see 1 Peter 5:8—"someone" in this verse implies a person who is alone).

Transformation looks different for each person. The only similarity is that we should look more like Christ and less like ourselves. If we're holding anything up other than the standard of Christ, we're forcing people to be imitators of us rather than God. This is extremely unbiblical and unhealthy. It's not our job to change people, or to even save people. Christ died to do those things. Our job is to walk with students, including gay students, as they journey toward God's identity and wholeness—whatever that may look like.

In ministering to gay teenagers, realize that most have a lot of baggage to process. Some may come from broken homes, where they don't have positive role models as parents. Some may have faced abuse—physical, sexual, emotional, or mental. Some may deal with bullying every day at school, on the bus, at home, at work, or even at youth group. Guys may have been told they are not real men because they're too effeminate—or girls may have been told they are not real women because they're too tomboyish. Many gay teenagers perceive God to be like their uninvolved parents or their mean-spirited peers.

I know I did. Because Christians bullied me in school, I perceived God to be an unfair bully, too. Because my relationship with my dad was strained, I had a hard time accepting God as a perfect, all-loving Father. Teenagers deal with these issues daily, and these issues need to be dealt with in a community where Christ is the center. I want to end this chapter with more thoughts from my friend Chris:

> This transformation isn't instantaneous though. There is a process, and it's a hard process because you're letting go of deep attachments. Many of these attachments were formed to survive painful experiences in your life. …

Before you can live in the new self, there's this middle space where you have nothing to hold onto. It's the dark night of the soul that Christians have talked about throughout church history. Look at any story of transformation in Scripture, and you'll see this middle space in the process. Joseph was in prison. Jacob was alone on a dark riverbank. Moses was in the wilderness 40 years. Elijah was in a cave. Jonah was in a whale. Jesus experienced it in the wilderness following his baptism. This middle space is a space of grieving and letting go of who you've been and making peace with no longer having any false external security to hold on to.

We have spent our lives constructing fig leaves and building our identity around things related to our mission and community. Let go of this security blanket of the pretend self in order to move to the new self, where you're comfortable in who you are in Jesus. It's such an amazing feeling to know you're loved for who you are and where you are, and to be in a place where there is nothing you can change about your life to be more loved than you already are. This new self will provide a new focus to your mission and a new way to relate in your community.[25]

I can relate to what Chris wrote. The middle space for me was the time between becoming a follower of Jesus and the first few years of my marriage. This time was uncomfortable, confusing, and challenging; however, the time was deeply beneficial to where I am today, as a Christian and as a family man. At times, the season of transformation was tedious and overwhelming, especially when things didn't move as quickly as I wanted. Dealing with situations from the past and present is never easy, such as wrongs done to you or habits you can't shake.

Sometimes, especially in my case, we can hinder the process by refusing to give up things we know we need to submit to God (such as addictions, unforgiveness, bitterness, and so on). While teenagers in this position don't need someone to police them, they do need a voice of reason speaking into their lives that is filtered through the compassion of Christ. Remember, transformation happens within community.

Belong. Believe. Be transformed. These are core values needed in every student ministry, and foundational pieces in our walk with Christ. As a youth worker, how will you implement these truths into your personal life, your ministry, and your teaching? How will you aggressively love and intentionally invest in gay people in your church and community?

CHAPTER 6:

YOUTH MINISTRY FAQS [AND QUESTIONS TO DISCUSS][26]

Below are additional questions I've received from youth workers, along with short versions of the answers I provided them.

I HAVE A GAY TEEN IN OUR MINISTRY. WHAT BOUNDARIES SHOULD I SET UP FOR THEM?

As we discussed in Chapters 3 and 4, the more proactively you set boundaries within your ministry, the better things will be. You don't want to be creating boundaries on the fly, so think through things carefully and fairly. As for PDA, you should hold gay teens to the same standard as straight teens. When arrangements need to be made for retreats and camps, it's good to have at least one adult in each room—especially in a room with a gay teen. This helps eliminate any false accusations or times for bullying to occur. The majority of gay teens won't try anything with other teens for fear of being bullied, unfriended, teased, and so on. So you shouldn't have to worry about anything sexual. If, however, you feel there's concern, pull the gay teen aside beforehand and discuss with him or her if sharing a room with certain people will be an issue. The conversation will be awkward for everyone involved, but it's something that should be done ahead of time and in private.

CHRISTIAN TEENS SEE NOTHING WRONG WITH THEIR GAY FRIENDS HAVING RELATIONSHIPS.
HOW DO I ADDRESS THIS?

It's true that the majority of Christian teens today see nothing wrong with their gay friends dating members of the same sex, and this is because teenagers today have a hard time separating their nice friends and the sin we talk about. In their minds the question is, "How can my friend, who is so nice to people, be considered evil and sinful because they're gay?" Their question is valid. Therefore, you need to address this carefully and compassionately. Remember the common ground approach we talked about earlier. All of us, no matter how good we may seem, need the salvation of Christ. No sin is greater than another (though consequences may vary), so through the cross we all come to Christ on level ground. The point isn't so much that their friend is gay, but if that friend knows Jesus, or where that friend needs help in growing closer to Jesus. Our focus is on pointing students to Jesus, and we allow him to work in the hearts and lives of those he calls us to love unconditionally.

A GAY FRIEND TOLD ME THAT HE HATES WHEN PEOPLE SAY HE AND HIS SEXUALITY ARE BROKEN.
HOW SHOULD I RESPOND?

Openly gay people who find nothing sinful with their homosexuality admittedly state, "We aren't broken." To some extent, they have a point. Some within the church have called gays and lesbians "broken"—a belief that they're considered less than human, they're damaged people, they're unlovable and must prove themselves to be accepted. In this sense, I fully agree with LGBT people that they are not broken; they're people made in God's image! In the other sense, however, there's truth. When people use "broken" to mean that we all fall short of God's glory and that sin has wrecked our relationships with God and others, then yes, we're all broken people in need of Jesus' redemption. This includes having a broken sexuality, which involves everyone. Sin has ruined the healthy view of sex and sexuality; it has turned both into objects of obsessions and addictions. We all need to allow Jesus to redeem our views concerning sex and sexuality so we see both from his perspective and not our own. Therefore, respond to your friend (or family member) with compassion, but also share the truth that we're all broken and need Jesus' redemption and restoration.

HOW DO I TALK ABOUT HOMOSEXUALITY AT YOUTH GROUP?

Talk about homosexuality openly and honestly. However, center this conversation on grace and mercy, and bathe it in prayer. Although it's good to discuss the truths and lies concerning homosexuality, I also suggest that youth workers talk about this issue within a broader series on healthy sexuality. How does God define sexuality? What does it mean to live a life of purity in relation to Christ? Whenever I teach on this subject, I focus on whole-life purity (what you watch, read, listen to, think about, speak about, and so on), instead of only focusing on one specific area. I would also invite someone who deals with same-sex attractions to share his or her story with your students. Personal experiences work great and help put a human face on the issue. Use the time afterward to help your students articulate their positions and beliefs, so that when the issue of homosexuality confronts them, they'll be able to handle themselves confidently and biblically. A word of caution: Make sure that during these times, you correctly handle reactions from the audience and those speaking. Don't allow name-calling, obscene gestures, and crude remarks to rear their ugly head. I would also get the permission of your senior pastor and leadership team before scheduling an event like this. Ask permission before needing to ask for forgiveness.

I NEED ADVICE ON PEOPLE IN LEADERSHIP WHO ARE GAY.

Using the same criteria as other situations, hold all leaders to the same standards, whether they're gay or straight. Let me state this bluntly: I believe same-sex attractions don't disqualify someone from leadership or ministry roles. When I was finding a ministry position after college, quite a few churches refused to look at my résumé because I openly shared my testimony. Despite my experience, references, and even my calling, they proceeded to hold my attractions at a greater value than everything else. This is failing to see the person as a new creation in Christ, and only looking at them as an uncomfortable issue.

The only problem I see in a gay individual taking a leadership position is if they hold a different theological belief about their sexuality than the church. If you eliminate someone from leadership just because of this issue that he or she struggles with, you need to eliminate those who wrestle with gossip, gluttony, lying, lust, and any other sin, which eliminates everyone from leadership roles—including you and me. But if the person in leadership wants to live out his or her attractions with the same-sex, then I think that person needs to be removed from leadership—just as we should respond to any person in leadership who willingly sins without repentance.

Help leaders succeed by providing training and accountability. Don't put the person in awkward positions, and do ask for their input on setting appropriate boundaries in order to help them avoid temptation snares—as every leader should have. If they're new to leadership roles, set them up with a mentor, or mentor them yourself. Listen to their struggles, pray with them and for them, and give them a chance to shine. Many qualified people with same-sex attractions are anxiously waiting to be the leader God has called them to be.

HOW DO I DEAL WITH A TRANSGENDER TEEN?

First, understand what *transgender* means. Here's how it's defined by one gay-rights organization: "Transgender is an umbrella term for people whose gender identity differs from what is typically associated with the sex they were assigned at birth. For transgender people, the sex they were assigned at birth and their own internal gender identity don't match. Most transgender people seek to bring their bodies more into alignment with their gender identity. People under the transgender umbrella may describe themselves using one (or more) of a wide variety of terms, including transgender, transsexual, and genderqueer. Always use the descriptive term preferred by the individual. Transgender people may or may not alter their bodies hormonally and/or surgically, and a transgender identity isn't dependent upon medical procedures. Transgender is an adjective, and should never be used as a noun."[27] I've found this definition to be helpful in my ministry and in steering my conversations with others.

Second, take this issue seriously. I personally have never struggled with my gender identity; however, I do know teenagers and adults who do, so this is a very real issue for the church. While researching this subject, I discovered that there are people who are born with the genetics of one sex yet have the physical appearance of the other. Some people don't fit this description but rather "feel" that they are to live as the opposite sex. I don't think we're in a position to judge which sex a student should be; rather, we are to love them regardless, as Jesus would.

MINISTRY QUESTIONS TO DISCUSS

Below are some questions designed for you to work through by yourself, as a youth ministry, and as a church. Don't just put down vague "church answers." Write out specific answers and steps. Search your heart and strive to discern what God is asking you to do—individually and as a ministry.

- What personal biases about the gay community do I need to work through?

- What are my fears, hopes, and expectations?

- What do I want God to do within the gay community?What am I willing to commit to, right now, in reaching out to the gay community?

- As a student ministry, how are we prepared to accept and deal with openly gay students?

- Is our student ministry a safe place? If not, how can we change things to make it one?

- How can we build a ministry that balances truth and grace?

- How are we talking about sexuality in general? How can we better talk about it?

- Do we allow time for honest discussions on sensitive topics? How can we improve this?

- How are we talking about homosexuality? Are we having honest discussions about it? How can we improve in this area?

- As a student ministry, how will we handle students coming out? [Or, how are we handling openly gay students currently in our ministry?]

- As a student ministry, how will we handle gay couples that come to our events? [Or, how are we handling openly gay couples currently in our ministry?]

- As a student ministry, how will we reach out to same-sex parents?

- How will we address gay students or adults wanting to participate in leadership roles? How will we address those who want to be leaders but hold to a different teaching about sexuality than our church holds?

- What training and resources do we need to make us more effective in reaching out to gay students?

- How are we praying for our gay students and their families within our church and community?

- How are we praying for gay parents within our church, student ministry, and community?

PART 3:

FAMILIES AND FRIENDS

CHAPTER 7:

LOVING YOUR GAY CHILD

If you're reading this book because you have a son or daughter who's gay, I'm thankful that you're taking the time to discover how you can effectively minister to this important person in your life. If you're a youth worker, senior pastor, or anyone else who's walking alongside a family or individual during this season of life, you'll still find this section of the book beneficial. And I encourage you to pass along these thoughts to people who will find them helpful.

I remember talking with my mom a few years ago, asking her why we didn't talk about my being gay. She simply replied: "I didn't know what to say. I didn't know how to help." Sadly, my mom's response resembles many other parents' responses. When a child comes out, the entire family is shaken up: *Where do we go from here? How will everyone else respond? What questions should I ask? What did I do wrong?*

While the territory is often uncharted and each family situation will be different, the venture is, surprisingly, not that difficult. In other words, it doesn't take a trained counselor to walk beside a friend who is dealing with having a gay child. What matters—more than any advice that one could give—is a supporting presence. This type of presence is highly needed for parents of a gay child because it lets them know that when all seems lost, at least one person is willing to take the time to understand and listen.

Nowhere is this presence needed more than within the church. Unfortunately, not only has the church been silent on how to minister to gays and lesbians, but we often have also failed to show a supportive presence in the life of a family with a gay son or daughter. Therefore, I want to offer some advice to you as parents, if you're walking this road.

TALKING WITH YOUR CHILD

After I came out to my parents, nothing more was asked or discussed about my sexuality. I know they had questions, and so did I, but no one really knew how to face the pink elephant in the room. In fact, I remember one night having a fight with a guy I was seeing. I stormed into the house and ran upstairs, and my mom began calling after me, "What's wrong?" I came down with some stuff to give back to my now ex-boyfriend, looked at her, and asked, "Do you really want to know?" We both looked at each other in silence. I walked away saying, "I didn't think so."

Was this her fault? No, I don't blame her—now. I did, for a long time. I hated the fact that my parents didn't want to know about what was *really* going on in my life at the time. However, looking back, they were really just as confused as I was about the whole thing. They didn't know what to say, how to say it, or when to say it. Almost all parents in this situation are just like my parents; they don't know how to react when their child says, "I'm gay." Christian parents *really* have a hard time with this discussion. How does one love their child unconditionally and still follow God faithfully? Can both even be done? I firmly believe that yes, both can be done. In fact, this is exactly what must be done in every parent/child relationship, no matter the outcome or the journey taken.

When your child approaches you to talk about their sexuality, they're coming with certain expectations already in place. They're expecting you to overreact, to yell, to argue with them, and maybe even throw them out. Your child is hoping these things don't happen, but they're prepared for them nonetheless. They're also hoping you'll accept their sexuality as they fully accept it. Most likely, your child has been wrestling with things for quite awhile, and now that they've accepted everything, they want you to accept everything, too. This is an unrealistic expectation on their part, as no parent is fully prepared to hear their son or daughter tell them they're gay. Still, my prayer for you is that you respond differently than they might be expecting.

As your child begins to tell you what they've been holding in for a long time, be sure to let them speak openly and honestly. This isn't a time to argue or a time to "fix" things; it's a time for you to listen to what they're saying (and not saying) about what they're dealing with. Whether you agree with their conclusions or not, you need to hear them out.

After they've finished talking, your child doesn't need to hear, "This is just a phase," or "You're not really gay; you're just really confused," or "You can change these feelings," or similar statements. Rather, they need to hear things like, "I still love you," and "I don't understand, but I'm going to try," and "We'll get through this." How you respond to your child now can determine how the rest of this journey goes. They'll remember your words for the rest of their life.

So in responding to your child, it's OK to ask questions, but watch that the questions don't cause your child to put up a wall. Two good questions would be, "How can I help you through this?" and "What do you need from me and your father/mother?" Reaffirm your love for them—this is what they're longing to hear from you. With that, reaffirm that things will be all right. Remember, even though your son or daughter may be telling you things with ease, inside they're a mess. They're expecting the worst to happen; prove them wrong!

It's perfectly normal to refrain from talking at length with your child about their recent news. In fact, if you need time to process things, tell them this. Either way, keeping an open communication with your child is very important and healthy. Author Mike Haley advises parents that "nothing is unhealthier [for you and your child] than denial and avoidance" of the issue at hand.[28] No matter how hard it may be to talk about it, you *must* eventually talk about things. Your child doesn't care so much if you understand 100 percent what they're experiencing as much as they desperately need you to talk with them and reaffirm your love for them—the unconditional kind of love. This may be hard at first, but understand this: God calls us to love regardless and to live truth through his grace. Above all else, remember that this is still your child. Also, know that affirming them doesn't mean you have to affirm how they choose to live their life.

TENDING YOUR HEART

As you're processing things, I urge you to be cautious of a few things personally. **First, don't blame yourself.** Almost all parents think it's their fault that their child is gay. While we all could be better parents in areas, your child's sexuality isn't your fault. As I stated earlier in this book, homosexuality is a deep and complex topic. Putting blame on yourself puts unwarranted guilt and shame on you, which causes this journey to be that much more cumbersome to walk. Stop blaming yourself!

If you've done something that may have caused some harm, seek the Lord's grace and mercy. In repenting, you're forgiven, and the burden is no longer yours to carry! Allow God to restore broken relationships and the broken hearts of all involved. If another person has caused harm, seek the Lord's strength to forgive the person, and to release the anger and bitterness you hold toward them. It would be wise to invite a pastor, Christian counselor, or trusted friend to walk with you through this process of letting go.

Second, don't give up on God. He has not forsaken you, nor has God forsaken your child—his child. In Romans 8:38-39, the Apostle Paul tells us that for those who are in Christ, nothing can separate us from the love of God. Your child's sexuality declaration did not catch God off-guard, nor does it stop God from loving him or her. Likewise, God isn't about to stop loving you either because you love your gay son or daughter. If we're in Christ, we're secure in Christ. For everything, God offers forgiveness; God's grace is limitless. There are three moments from the ministry of Christ that I love and use in ministry to parents and gay teenagers: the woman at the well (John 4), the woman caught in adultery (John 8), and the prodigal son (Luke 15). These passages exemplify greatly what I'm sharing here.

Third, make sure you grieve in healthy ways. It's OK to get mad, and it's OK to cry. Going through a grieving process is healthy, because parents don't raise kids hoping they'll one day come out and confess they're gay. In your grieving, there's a loss of what you probably had hoped your child would eventually become: married with kids. Each parent will go through their own stages of guilt, shame, anger, loss, and acceptance on their terms. Don't force your spouse, but make sure he or she is getting out emotions in some kind of healthy venue, too.

In going through these stages, it's important that you have a person or a group to walk alongside you. If you have a church family, let them know what is going on, once you feel safe and ready. You cannot make this type of journey alone. Just as your kids need support, you need it, too. I cannot stress enough the importance of finding people to talk with, either face to face or through technology (email, social media, phone). The more you bottle things up, the harder things will be for everyone.

Fourth, examine your expectations. A word to the wise: Forced counseling won't work. While some counseling would be good for family and relationship reasons, forcing your child to see a counselor in order to make them straight can be pointless and harmful. What will work are mentoring, prayer, personal spiritual growth, and healthy interactions with members of the same sex. Remember, the entire point of "change" is to become like Christ—nothing more and nothing less. As we grow closer to the heart of God the Father, God begins transforming us into who he desires us to be.

Your job as a parent is to not convict, condemn, or change your child. Conviction and change come from the Spirit. While there's no condemnation for those in Christ (Romans 8:1), God does desire to transform us with his grace and truth. For me, change happened only when I stopped trying to achieve my own expectations and began to desire God's will for my life—no matter what that looked like. All in Christ undergo transformation. However, it will happen in God's timing, it will happen as long as your child allows it, and it won't happen by force or by seeking after your own expectations.

Fifth, allow God to transform you. In the middle of God transforming your child, understand that he is going to be transforming you as well. One thing I've learned as a parent is that when I teach or quote a passage to my kids, I'd better be prepared to hear it first myself. In hearing it, I've to apply it, too. The same is true for you: Before quoting or sharing Scriptures with your child, be sure you've taken them to heart yourself first. You may feel you've a right to call them out for failing to live by God's standards, but can they call you out, too?

Allow humility, compassion, and God's Spirit to guide you. Approach this journey with sober judgment and genuine love, rejoicing in hope, remaining patient in tribulation, staying constant in prayer, living in harmony with others, and overcoming evil with good (Romans 12:3-21). Seek after God's counsel. Ask him to break your heart for your child and their friends. Ask God to help you see your child through his eyes, and to love your child through his heart. *And whatever you do, in word or deed, do everything in the name of the Lord Jesus, giving thanks to God the Father through him (Colossians 3:17).*

The more you give God the entire situation, the stronger you'll become in walking through this journey. As for your son or daughter, God's kindness will lead them back to him (Romans 2:4)—and as for you, God's grace is sufficient, for God's power is made perfect in your weakness (2 Corinthians 12:9-10). Rest in these truths. Don't give up or lose hope. Continue loving your child and continue trusting in your Savior.

IN THEIR WORDS

Over the years, I've talked with hundreds of parents on the same journey as you. I've asked some of them to share personal wisdom and experiences with you. Each parent's story is different—some teenagers and adults are still living in gay relationships, while others have submitted their life and sexuality to Christ.

NORA, FRED, AND BETH

Nora and Fred are the parents of Beth, who at 21 came out to her parents as a lesbian. Nora offers some advice she learned during this 24-year journey, noting that she and Fred struggled alone during this time because "we were too shamed to share our fears and grief with others." Beth is now a Christian, living a celibate life, with her daughter. Nora, Fred, and Beth all serve in ministry to families of gay individuals. Nora shares these additional points:

- **God and you come first.** The greatest lesson we learned through these times was that we must decrease, and Christ must increase. Staying connected with him is our first priority.

- **Hug your child. Parents,** please touch, hug, and love your child without conditions.

- **Compassion is central.** My husband, Fred, learned that confrontation was not always the answer; rather, compassion toward Beth went a long way. Don't drive your loved one away, but be interested in their feelings, their concerns, and even their friends. Remember, their friend is someone's child, too.

- **Dad, your child needs you.** Dads, I want you to know you're greatly needed in your child's life. Not every son and daughter has to fit a mold that we call normal. Help them embrace their uniqueness, and encourage them to flourish in the talents God has given them. They greatly need you and your affirmation.

- **Don't neglect community.** Fred and I had no support during our 24-year journey. We, like so many, tried to keep that "Sunday smile" while our hearts were breaking. This isn't what God wants for his people. Christians are to share each other's burdens. Find a support group where you can express your concerns and know others will walk with you through your pain.

- **Maintain your marriage.** Fred and I needed each other, and you'll need your spouse, too. Look for things you can do together to just have fun. Don't lose your ability to laugh, and, by all means, don't let this issue control your life. Life does go on, and it's important that your marriage stand strong.

- **Journal your journey.** It might surprise you what God has in mind for you. It certainly surprised me.

Nora further shared that "a happy ending isn't always promised to us parents, especially while on this particular journey. However, God remains faithful and steadfast. Nothing will change the love you have for your child, and nothing will change God's love for them either."

I asked Beth to share the three most important things her parents showed her during this time. Here's what she said: *At the end of every conversation, my mom would always say, "Honey, Jesus loves you." I'd say, "I* know, Mom." My parents also never stopped praying for me. They knew I needed the Lord and the Lord's protection. Best of all, my parents never stopped loving me or showing me their love. My siblings were a different story, though; but my parents' love never wavered.

JUDY

Judy and her husband have a gay child and help minister to parents of gay individuals. She says this: *Love them! Form a prayer team, pray, and take care of your marriage and yourselves. Join a support group if you can. If not, join an online group. The most practical thing I've done is be intentional in educating myself in what my children are interested in, so that I can communicate with them on subjects other than homosexuality.*

MARA-LEE

Mara-lee and I currently sit on the board for Hope for Wholeness,[29] and she offers these thoughts on the relationship with her gay daughter: *My advice to parents is to remember you've history with this beloved child! She was your treasure when freshly born, your beauty when she was 3, your laughing princess when she was 9, your quirky tween, your tenacious girl in high school. She didn't become a freak of nature. She's still her, just a little more revealed than what you saw before. I told my daughter, "I've never been a mother of a lesbian before! I'm going to hurt you, and so please forgive me when I mess up." Well, truthfully, I've always been a mother of a lesbian!! It just wasn't revealed to me yet, and I loved her then. I can surely love her now. We have memories, some are bad, but lots are good! I needed to repent to my daughter for the things God revealed to me—and continues to reveal—that I did poorly. I needed to accept*

*forgiveness before his throne for my faults, and then
keep building good memories with my daughter. By
God's great grace, I'm ready to be one of the shoulders
my daughter comes and cries out her pain on. And I
believe she will, because I stayed around, I loved her,
and I built upon her wholeness in every way.*

CHAPTER 8:

LOVING A GAY SIBLING OR FRIEND

If you're reading this book because you have a sibling or friend who's gay, I'm thankful that you're taking the time to discover how you can effectively minister to this important person in your life. If you're a youth worker, senior pastor, or anyone else who's walking alongside a family or individual during this season of life, you'll still find this section of the book beneficial. And I encourage you to pass along these thoughts to people who will find them helpful.

I receive a growing number of emails from siblings of LGBT people. Some want to understand their brother or sister and want to reach out in love and support, while keeping true to their beliefs. Other siblings want nothing to do with their brother or sister, feeling betrayed by them. In these situations, usually the parents are the ones who email me asking for advice on how to bring peace to their family.

For me, this was never an issue, because I didn't actually come out to my siblings—I'm seven years older than my next brother. When I first came out, I felt they were too young to understand. As we all grew older, I felt it still wasn't an issue to discuss; looking back, however, I wish we had talked.

Though the discussion may be uncomfortable, I think it's a conversation siblings need to have with one another. For those coming out, the age of younger siblings needs to be considered, and timing really is everything. For those receiving the news, do so in a posture of empathy, and be praying for guidance as your brother or sister fills you in on a part of their life that's been hidden in secret. You aren't required to gain full understanding from this one conversation, and it's foolish to think you won't be emotional afterward. Things need to be processed, and you need to have more conversations with your sibling. As you go through these times, here are some suggestions.

- **Listen.** Hear what your brother or sister is saying, and hear what they are not saying. Try to understand what is being shared, knowing that understanding doesn't mean you have to agree with everything. Give your full attention to your sibling, and try to clear your mind of questions, rebuttals, and condemnation. Listen with your ears and your eyes.

- **Be honest.** The uncomfortable part of this interaction is the honesty and vulnerability, yet these things are so vital to conversations like this. Let your sibling know they're free to talk honestly with you. Allow them to share their experiences and understanding of things. When they have finished, ask if you can share your honest thoughts with them. While you can state a difference in your beliefs about homosexuality, this isn't a time for a theological debate. Share your heart, fears, concerns, and questions. Let them know where you're coming from. However, allow them to answer you, and be ready to accept their answers—right or wrong. Their answers state where they are, just as yours state where you are. You have a right to your opinion, as do they, so neither should try to convince the other of fully embracing their position. It's OK to disagree, and it's OK to be on the opposite ends of the spectrum. How you live within this disagreement matters more. In everything, be an example of Christ. Find the common ground, stand upon it, and return to it after disagreeing.

- **Embrace.** When the conversation finishes, hug your sibling. Reaffirm your love for them, even if you don't feel love toward them at that moment. You are still brother and sister. Though they may feel like a stranger to you, you're still family. Sure, in some ways things will be different, but largely nothing has changed. Continue doing activities you've done before, continue to hang out, continue to have lunch, continue to be part of each other's lives. One of the greatest things your sibling needs now is the love of their family. Be that presence for them. Regarding boundaries, some might need to be set, but be sure to set realistic and Christ-honoring ones. Some situations will be uncomfortable. Press through them together. If you're older and have your own family, you, your spouse, and your sibling need to discuss whether or how to tell your own kids. There is no need to hide your kids from your sibling or to exclude them from family functions, unless serious issues arise.

- **Focus on Jesus.** Remember to keep him at the center of everything. If your brother or sister doesn't know Jesus, this is priority No. 1. If your sibling is already a Christian, then help them deepen their relationship with Jesus. Your job isn't to convict them or condemn them. Your job is to be a willing vessel of God's truth, mercy, and grace. Seek his leading and follow his example.

LOVING YOUR FRIEND

Regarding friends, let me say that gay people need friends they can trust in and turn to when life gets heavy. In late August 2000, as I was holed up in my apartment, dealing with deep depression and the heaviness of the secrets I was holding in, my good friends Pete, Carolanne, and Laura schemed a plan to "kidnap" me and take me to a place where we could talk about everything. And they wanted to know *everything* that was going on with me. At a picnic table in the park, they sat and listened to me spill my guts about everything I was hiding: my same-sex attractions, my doubts with God, my hookups, my fears, and everything in between.

While I hated their scheming and went unwillingly, it was a huge turning point in my life. After we were all done and exhausted from talking, each friend embraced me, with Pete hugging me the longest. Their affirmation, especially from Pete, was greatly needed, greatly received, and greatly healing for me. In my biased opinion, gay people need these types of friends. God has used so many people to influence my life, and so many relationships have taught me huge lessons in life—how to love, how to be a man, how to lead a family, how to smile, and so on. Friendships are vital in this journey:

Here are some specific thoughts and tips if you're walking alongside a friend during this journey.

- **Be Jesus to your friend.** This is what your friend needs more than anything else. You have the privilege and honor of loving your friend like Jesus loves him or her.

- **Be patient with your friend.** There will be some ups and downs in this journey. Walk beside them.

Celebrate their victories, and pray with them when defeats come. Extend the same amount of grace to them that God extends to you.

- **Be trustworthy.** True friends are there for each other no matter what. You may have to make an effort to keep in contact. You don't have to be a doormat, but keep your door open to them whenever they come around. It's wise to keep things healthy, and they shouldn't consume every minute of your day. But if they need to chat, make time. If they need to vent, listen. And if they need to cry, comfort them.

- **Be communal.** When you gather with straight friends for a fun event, don't leave out your gay friends. Help them to belong, to be a part of authentic community. Gain their perspective on things: what they need, what areas they're struggling with, how you can support them, and so on. Sometimes before hanging out, ask them to pick the event or meeting place. In your friendship, remember that Christ is central; walk beside them in being a disciple of Jesus. Love them regardless of what attractions they have or what beliefs they hold.

- **Be a prayer warrior.** Through the years, I've become greatly aware of how the prayers and intercession of others have influenced my walk with Christ. From Yvonne praying for me to know Christ, to Pete praying I would realize how much God loved me, to Craig who intercedes for me when trials come, friends praying regularly for one another fulfills the command to carry each other's burdens (Galatians 6:2).

- **Be educated.** Whether you're a sibling or a friend, the topic of Scripture and homosexuality will eventually arise in your conversations. Get educated about the issues and try to understand or at least familiarize yourself with both sides. Six:11 Ministries offers great resources (from myself and others) on our website (six11.wordpress.com). The more you know, the better you'll be able to handle things. When discussing Scripture, take a stand based on your convictions, but listen to your friend's view, too. The point isn't to win an argument or to present the best scriptural case for why you're right (this goes for both sides). The point is to stay friends in spite of your differences. Present the character of Jesus in every word and deed (see 1 Peter 3:15-16). The more we heed to his promptings, the less we'll mess things up by listening to ourselves.

CHAPTER 9:

FAMILY FAQS
(AND QUESTIONS TO DISCUSS)[30]

Below are common questions parents have asked over the years via my blog and ministry, six11.wordpress.com.

I THINK MY CHILD IS GAY.
WHAT SHOULD I DO?

As a Christian, you shouldn't do anything without first praying. So start by taking a deep breath and praying. Then I would really process why you think your child is gay: mannerisms, interests, associations, or sexual activity. If it's one of the first three, I wouldn't jump the gun and say your child is gay if he likes art or she likes sports. Many teenagers today like different things, and they're simply trying to figure out who they are. I would be more concerned if your child is getting into same-sex relationships or sexual activity (porn or sex). If this is the case, see below. If it's not the case, talk with your child and invest time into their world, whether you can relate to their interests or not. The more time you invest in what they care about, the more they'll be open to you about who they are.

I CAUGHT MY SON
VIEWING GAY PORN. HELP!

If your child is viewing porn—gay or straight—then you need to help put a stop to their access. Whether you need to move the computer into a centralized place, install a Web blocker or Internet accountability software, or get rid of Internet access all together, as the parent you have full authority to control what your teen is viewing online. Viewing porn, especially gay porn, won't necessarily make your child gay, but it will cause same-sex attractions to increase, particularly if same-sex attractions already heavily exist. It would be best to confront your teen, preferably by the parent of the same gender, as quickly as possible instead of allowing their actions to continue. Here are two great websites to connect with regarding this issue: xxxchurch.com and covenanteyes.com.

WHAT DO WE TELL OUR OTHER CHILDREN ABOUT THEIR GAY BROTHER/SISTER?

It would be good to sit down with your other children and discuss what's going on with their sibling. Some counselors say to do this without your gay child around, and others suggest doing the opposite. I believe both options are OK to do. The main point is to talk openly about the situation. Make it a safe place for conversation, and allow your children to express their emotions, questions, and other reactions. Assure them that their sibling is still the same person they've always known, and that your love for them doesn't and won't change. Do they have a right to know? Yes, especially if your children are close relationally and in age.

HOW DO WE DEAL WITH OTHER FAMILY MEMBERS' REJECTION OR FEARS?

My grandma told me that after I'd told my dad I was gay, he called up his family and told them that "Shawn is gay, and if you have a problem with this, you'll deal with me." My dad never told me this (I wish he had), but his words meant a lot to his family and to me. First, his message told the family their job wasn't to accept or reject my decision; rather, it was to love me as he loved me. If anyone had a problem with my being gay, they were to express their concerns through him, not with me. Secondly, by doing this it showed them—and even more, me—that I was his son, no matter what. I think parents would be wise to convey the same message to their family members.

MY SON SAYS WE'RE TOO JUDGMENTAL. WE HAVE AFFIRMED OUR UNCONDITIONAL LOVE FOR HIM BUT CANNOT APPROVE OF HIS CHOICE. WE NEED SOME GUIDANCE.

Children, including teenagers, want to be totally accepted by their parents. When a parent shows disapproval toward a decision, the child is often offended and takes it personally. This is especially true for people who are gay and whose parents don't approve of their decision to pursue a gay identity. Some parents totally shut out their gay child and refuse to amend anything until the child ceases to be gay. Flat out, this is a wrong and costly position to take. Some parents are able to fully embrace their child's sexuality and look past what Scripture has to say about the situation. I feel this is a wrong position to take as well. Other parents unconditionally love their son or daughter, while choosing not to condone their child's decision to pursue a gay identity. Sons and daughters in this situation may take offense at this and accuse parents (or other family members) of being judgmental. In this situation, I believe the parents are right and the child is wrong.

Not every decision he or she makes will be a good one, and parents have every right to not agree with a child's wrong decision. The task at hand for your gay teenager is that they understand this and respect this, just as they expect you to understand and respect them. Showing unconditional love to your teen doesn't mean supporting everything they say and do; it means you love them regardless of the good and bad decisions they make.

WHAT ROLE DOES A FATHER PLAY IN EVERYTHING?

Both males and females look to their dads for affirmation. It matters what our fathers think about us and about the decisions we make. We want our dads to be proud of us. Therefore, the role of a father is huge within every child's life. The struggle for most dads is expressing feelings openly and honestly with others, especially their sons and daughters. However, this vulnerable exchange needs to happen. As I mentioned earlier, not every son is going to play football and chase girls, and not every daughter is going to love cooking and dress pretty for boys. Some kids will behave differently, and fathers need to be OK with this—even accepting of this.

While a child has a part to play in this interaction, I believe responsibility rests with the dad to engage his children where they are, rather than where he wants them to be—whether his expectations are intentional or not. Fathers need to hug their sons and hold their daughters, affirming them both as the person they are and the person they're growing up to be. As Judy shared with us at the end of Chapter 7, parents need to be intentional about educating themselves in what their children are interested in, which will no doubt stretch the comfort zone of many parents. However, this stretching causes the parent/child relationship to be healthier and stronger.

HELP, MY DAUGHTER HAS A GIRLFRIEND!

Gay teenagers want to feel accepted and loved for who they are. As they walk through the halls at school, they see their friends holding hands with those they love, and gay students want to do the same thing. Therefore, it shouldn't be a surprise if your son or daughter comes home and says they're now dating someone. Fair questions to ask yourself include, *"How do I handle their dating relationship?"* and *"What boundaries do I set into place?"* A simplified answer is to establish the same boundaries you would create if your child were dating a member of the opposite sex. It's your house, and you have the right to lay down specifics about relationships, people coming over, sleepovers, parties, and so on. However, I would make two big cautions. Not every gay teen is interested in having sex; they mainly just want some normalcy in their life through friends. Second, the same rules you apply to your gay daughter should be the same rules you apply to your straight children, too.

HOW DO I SET BOUNDARIES FOR MY GAY CHILD?

All kids need boundaries. As parents, we should create boundaries that not only give protection to our teenagers, but also help them develop Christlike character as they grow into adulthood. Boundaries must have a point and go beyond, "Because I said so." If both parents are present in the home, both should be personally involved with creating these boundaries and enforcing them; otherwise, the child will have the ability to pit one parent against another. (This dynamic changes, of course, with blended families, single-parent households, and families where grandparents or guardians are raising a teenager—but the underlying principle remains.) Regarding your gay teenager, the boundaries set for them should be the same boundaries set for your other children. If there's a dating age, apply this rule to all of your children. If there are restrictions on who can be in their bedrooms, apply this to everyone. The same goes for curfews, sleepovers, outings with friends, and the like. Set up boundaries based on your Christian standards, rather than your child's homosexuality.

Although sexual activity is a real concern, know that it's a real concern for every teenager, not just those who are gay. Not every gay teen is sex-crazed. Most gay teens are afraid and shy about getting sexual with another person. Therefore, in establishing boundaries for your child, be sure to make them realistic and not based on fear. More than anything, your gay teen wants to be a normal teenager—so let them be one. If there's cause for concern, address the issue with your son or daughter. Don't assume anything, unless you've hard evidence; rather, engage your child by talking about your concerns openly and honestly. Ask them what realistic boundaries they would set in place for themselves. Sometimes involving them in the boundary-making process allows them to know the level of trust you've in them. Remind them that when trust is broken, there are consequences—privileges are taken away, friends are restricted, and so on. If fear about the unknown still grips you, begin hosting hangout times, sleepovers, and other events and activities at your house. Before each gathering, pray; during the gathering, pray. Set the atmosphere in your home, because it's *your* home. Tolerance goes both ways.

MY CHILD IS GETTING BULLIED IN SCHOOL. WHAT SHOULD I DO?

If your child is getting bullied in school because he or she is gay, lesbian, bisexual, or transgender, then approach the principal and school board about the problem—and don't quit until a tangible solution has been carried out. The issue of bullying is a raging problem right now, and this is especially true for gay students. To ignore the complaints from your child about being bullied—or to brush them off as "just a phase that will pass"—will do more harm than good to your child. Some gay teenagers have killed themselves over being bullied; bullying isn't just an issue that will pass, so you need to take action.

IS IT INEVITABLE THAT MY GAY SON WILL GET AIDS OR KILL HIMSELF?

There are tons of reports out there about gay people—some correct and some incorrect. Yes, AIDS still exists within the gay population. However, if your son (or daughter) is careful and monogamous in their relationships, they're less likely to get AIDS than if they weren't. As for suicide, yes, chances do increase for gay teens over straight teens. However, if you provide a safe, open, and unconditional loving environment for your child, then the chance of them committing suicide lessens. Of course, not every gay person gets AiDS or commits suicide. A lot depends on the family structure and support they have standing behind them. Cover your child in prayer, and raise them in the love and understanding of Christ, and he will handle the rest.

IF MY GAY CHILD ACTS UPON THEIR SAME-SEX ATTRACTIONS, ARE THEY STILL A CHRISTIAN?

This is a heated and heavy question. Scripture tells us that it's by grace we have been saved (Ephesians 2:8-10), and that our lives should mirror the way Jesus lived (Ephesians 5:1). For those of us in Christ, we're God's adopted children, saints, and servants. Nothing can separate us from these things (Romans 8:37-39). The Bible is full of many examples of people participating in sinful actions; the majority of them did not lose their position with God or in Christ because of their sin. However, Scripture also warns us of grieving the Holy Spirit and living against the ways of God. We are his children and have been set apart from the world. Your child being openly gay doesn't forfeit their salvation, but it does put into question their commitment to Christ. I wouldn't cast any stones; rather, I'd continue praying that God's hand would continue to lead your child closer to him.

MY GAY SON IS GETTING MARRIED AND WANTS US TO ATTEND THE WEDDING. SHOULD WE GO?

I receive this question a lot from parents, especially with the legalization of gay marriage in many states. Here's the easy part of my answer: Do whatever God is asking you to do. If God says go, then follow his prompting in trust. If God says don't participate, then follow his lead. The hard part of this answer, of course, is figuring out what choice God is asking you to make. It's my personal belief that God won't chastise you or send you to hell because you attended your gay son's wedding (though there are parents who think they'll go to hell for attending such a wedding—sometimes because their pastor said so). Whether you go or stay home, my prayer is that you represent Jesus through your actions and words. Don't go to the wedding looking to convert people, or even to change the mind of your child. Go to be a visible witness of Christ, praying all the while that he would intervene, soften hearts, and work in the lives of those in attendance. You never know how God is going to use you as his witness, unless you step out in faith and walk forward.

FAMILY QUESTIONS TO DISCUSS

Below are some questions designed for you to work through as a family. Don't just put down vague "Christian answers." Write out specific answers and steps. Search your heart and strive to discern what God is asking of your family.

- As a family, how will we talk about biblical sexuality?

- As parents, what will we teach our kids about homosexuality?

- As parents, how will we teach our kids to respond to gay peers?

- How will I respond if my son or daughter comes out? What are my fears?

- What are my hopes and expectations for my child?

- Am I willing to let go and to trust God?

- How am I dealing with my child being gay?

- How do I interact or respond to my child's gay friends?

- How is our home a safe place? How can we make it a safer place?

- What does my support system look like? Where do I need additional help, and how will I seek out this help?

- What type of support is my child receiving? What additional help does he or she need? [Not what help *you* think your child needs, but what help he or she truly needs.]

- How is my family dealing with my child being gay?

- How is my child dealing with family members knowing that he or she is gay?

- How will we, as a family, respond to gay relatives? What will we tell our kids, and what type of response will we have concerning our kids and those relatives?

- Are our conversations with those relatives open and honest, balanced in truth and grace? Have we built bridges or created divides?

- As a family, are we praying for our gay relatives, friends, neighbors, and co-workers? How are we praying, and what are we praying? Are we seeking God's heart and wholeness for them?

- How are we allowing God to use us in these situations? Are we open or closed to God's prompting?

PART 4:

RESPONDING WELL

CHAPTER 10:

THE CHURCH AS A RESTORATIVE COMMUNITY

It's one thing to reshape a student ministry to be a safe place where LGBT teenagers can come and experience Jesus. It's another thing to help a larger church community refocus itself in being a safe place. Therefore, it's very important for the entire leadership team of a church to lead and carry this vision, in order to effectively minister to gay teenagers and adults. I want to share some areas you need to wrestle with and process through, then give suggested answers and ideas that you and your church leadership can implement in your congregation.

UNDERSTAND THE CHURCH'S CALLING (BEYOND THE "COME TO US" MENTALITY)

What does Jesus expect from the church? Simply put, I believe he expects us to imitate his persona, ministry, and mission. In John 8:12, Jesus proclaimed that he is the light of the world, while in Matthew 5:14, he said that his followers are the light of the world. Even before he commissioned us, Jesus called his followers to live, think, love, and respond with his character and likeness. Jesus calls us to follow his example: to teach people everything he's taught us by modeling his likeness, to love them as he loves us, to see them as he sees us, and to serve them as he has served us.

As we begin to model Christ, I think it's wise that we admit our wrongs and recognize that things need to change. Put yourself into the shoes of a gay person stepping into your church for the first time: *What are some fears or preconceived notions that person might have? Will that person feel welcomed or feel like an outsider?* I was very leery of the church when I first came to Christ. I felt as if I had the word *homo* written across my forehead, and that anyone who saw me saw this label primarily. Though I was wrong in this assumption about some people, it was still a real perception to me. Honestly, at times I still feel this way when I walk into new Christian circles (including churches and small groups)—especially if I know that people have heard my story before.

I love the story of the prodigal son in Luke 15. When I speak to churches about ministering to the gay community, I often use this parable in my teaching because it gives a great picture of how the church, gay people, and God all interact with each other. My goal is to help Christians see how the father (representing God) responded to the younger brother (representing a gay individual), and to encourage Christians to act like the father instead of the older brother from the story.

Here's what I mean: When the younger brother realized he was better off back with his father, he developed a plan filled with false assumptions. He assumed his father would act a certain way, so he prepared for such a response. In many cases, when a gay person comes to church, he or she arrives with assumptions, too:

- They're scared of being thrown out, because people no longer consider them a son or daughter of the family.

- They come with predetermined punishments, expectations, attitudes, and reactions (most based on previous experiences).

- They come wanting life-change, but they're not ready to go as fast as the church wants.

- They come feeling worthless and undeserving, expecting Christians to want them to feel this way—and many Christians do.

I've talked with a lot of people—one just today, in fact—who feel betrayed and unwanted by the church because they have same-sex attractions. For them, it's healthier to stay detached from a church than to connect with one. These are real assumptions from people we cannot ignore. Likewise, we cannot ignore our wrongdoings as the "older brother":

- We have failed at times to see the bigger story of God.

- We have "done ministry" without being ministers of reconciliation.

- We have expected more from others without expecting more from ourselves.

- We have neglected to offer others the same grace, love, and forgiveness afforded to us by Jesus.

This doesn't make us hate-filled and mean-spirited people; rather, this should cause us to step upon the level ground of the cross with our fellow brothers and sisters. We all need the love of the Father; we all need his grace and mercy; none of us is righteous and deserving of the gift God gives. And yet he does, freely (see Romans 3:9-10, 22-24). This is the beauty of words found later in the New Testament: *Mercy triumphs over judgment (James 2:13).*

AGGRESSIVELY LOVE OTHERS (BEYOND THE CASUAL "HOW ARE YOU?")

Looking again at the prodigal son parable, our posture toward those who deal with same-sex attractions should resemble that of the father. I believe Jesus presents a beautiful picture of God the Father. The son returns just as he is—covered in pig manure, tattered and torn clothing, tired, hungry, shameful—yet the father passionately welcomes his son. Just as importantly, the father saw his son from a far distance, indicating that he was constantly on the lookout for his son's return. So when he spots the young man, the father runs toward him, arms open wide. The father isn't put off by his son's smell, appearance, or past behavior. All that the father sees is his son, who was once lost but is now found. The father doesn't see a problem to be fixed or a project to be conquered; he sees a person to be loved. Churches must imitate this posture when a gay, lesbian, bisexual, or transgender person comes through their doors.

As we talked about in Chapter 5, fulfilling Romans 12:13 (practicing hospitality) requires us to aggressively love others toward Christ. We do this by developing relationships with people. We do this by investing time into a person's life. We do this by listening to their story, seeing them beyond the problem, affirming them for who they are, and making it known to them that they're welcome to stay within our church community. When the son returned to his father, he came back expecting to be a slave for his father. Without hesitation, the father dressed the man in his rightful clothes and acknowledged him as his son by placing the family ring on his finger.

Aggressively loving someone is risky, costly, and radical. It takes time for walls to fall down within a person and for certain habits to cease. Just as Jesus was patient with you, so you must be patient with others. I love how Thom and Joani Schultz end their discussion on radical hospitality in their newest book: "In an age of 'instant everything,' remember that radical hospitality takes time. Be willing to invest in someone's life for the long haul. Embracing the maxim 'You're welcome just as you are' means trusting God's timing, purposes, and processes. Just as it takes time for a tree to grow, for fine wine to age—for any masterpiece to be created—relationships developed through radical hospitality (aggressive love) take time. The bottom line of radical hospitality: Be a friend. Don't even think about what a *church* should do. Do what *friends* would do."[31]

RETHINK THE ENDPOINT (BEYOND COOKIE-CUTTER CHRISTIANS)

Both brothers in the parable of the prodigal son expected their father to shell out a severe punishment for the wrongdoings of the younger son. Both were amazed at what the father did and did not do—he blew their expectations out of the water. While the younger son saw the great mercy of this act, the older brother was furious: *How could he forgive my brother for everything he's done against us?* The father tried to explain his reasoning but could not convince the older son that grace needed to be given and that the bigger picture needed to be seen: His brother was dead but is alive again. How much more do we as the body of Christ need to let go of our personal expectations for gays and lesbians?

What you think people need to hear isn't always what they actually need to hear. James gives wise words for us to consider: *Let every person be quick to hear, slow to speak, slow to anger (James 1:19).* When listening, we need to be attentive to what the person is saying to us and what God is saying to us. In hearing people, we begin to see people. In hearing people through the ears of God, we begin to see people through the eyes of God. Jesus did this well, and it didn't matter who the person was. He looked upon people with compassion, even people who rejected him (see Jesus' examples in Matthew 15:32 and Mark 10:21).

We've become a culture that speaks first and listens second; this needs to be reversed. Yes, we have something to say and we have a hope to offer, but we must earn the right to be heard by people who've been hurt by others with the same message. We earn this right by building relationships with people and listening before speaking.

When speaking truth, do so in the manner of love and compassion. Pastors must teach biblical sexuality but must address their teachings to everyone, not just those who struggle with same-sex attractions. Teach about the design and the beauty of sex from God's perspective, and don't just speak against the evils of homosexuality. Nothing is harder for a gay person than to sit through a sermon where either the pastor makes fun of gay people or identifies homosexuality to be the sin above all other sins. If you or someone you know is doing this, please stop. Pastors need to shepherd those who are gay in their congregations, just as they need to shepherd other members. In the same mindset, pastors need to take seriously John 10:15-16—*I lay down my life for the sheep. And I have other sheep that aren't of this fold. I must bring them also, and they'll listen to my voice.* Christians with same-sex attractions are a part of the flock, because they belong to the Shepherd.

When speaking on homosexuality, try to stay away from making it a cut-and-dried issue, or one that is political. Understand that the conversation about homosexuality is at times complex and involves real people—people who may be sitting in front of you on Sunday morning. This isn't to say you shouldn't talk about the issue from a biblical point of view—by all means, please do. However, be cautious of the tone used, the words chosen, and the focus of the message. Give glory to Christ, and challenge the body to embrace those who are struggling and in need of authentic hope.

In addition, don't focus on the sin of a few while ignoring the sin of others. One of the biggest arguments from the gay community is that while churches stand up for the sanctity of marriage, divorces and affairs continue to go unchecked within the local church. Standing for marriage means standing for every marriage within your congregation and those around you in need of help. In a sense, we're showing favoritism—calling out one sin and ignoring others, and the New Testament speaks loudly against such practice (see James 2:1-13).

The ending point of our Christian walk isn't to be a follower of a religion, but to be a disciple of Jesus Christ. With the good news of Jesus as our foundation, we press on toward knowing Jesus and making him known, beyond our own desires and will. The Apostle Paul threw aside everything taught to him and all the privileges he had attained, in order to gain more of Christ, and we're called to do no less (see Philippians 3:7-16). When befriending and walking beside those who are gay, we present this goal, knowing that it's the same goal we're pursuing ourselves. We in the church must be careful to not offer unattainable expectations. We are to become men and women who seek after God's own heart, and however that looks for each individual needs to be OK.

Every person is unique, made for God's purposes, and the gifts we have—both natural and spiritual—don't have to match up with the cultural norm for that gender. Celebrate the unique gifts and talents of those within your congregation.

Another false expectation is assuming that marriage is for everyone. Some people with same-sex attractions are able to eventually pursue marriage with the opposite sex (like me). However, other Christians who identify as gay aren't able to marry. It's not because they don't want to get married; it's because they are not attracted to the opposite sex. Instead of letting them feel pressured into dating someone or even marrying someone, the church needs to walk beside such individuals and affirm their choice of staying celibate.

The church has pushed this path aside for too long. Celibate Christians aren't second-class Christians. They're a part of the body, as any other Christian is. If a person chooses to remain celibate, for whatever reason, their church community must arise to support them—period. As Paul put it: *Therefore encourage one another and build one another up (1 Thessalonians 5:11).*

CULTIVATE AUTHENTIC COMMUNITY
(BEYOND BIBLE STUDY)

Unity of the church is a common theme within the New Testament. The Apostle Paul offers this challenge: *If one member suffers, **all suffer together;** if one member is honored, **all rejoice together** (1 Corinthians 12:26, emphases added).* I love the truth Paul paints here for the church: We are in this together; none of us is alone in this journey of knowing Christ. The Marine slogan "Leave no one behind" comes to mind when reading this verse. Yet if we're honest, we struggle with cultivating authentic community within our churches. It may be a value to us, but far too often, little effort goes into living this value out. People desperately desire to be known and to be loved for who they are, not for who they are supposed to be. I'm convinced this truth lives within communities that see and love *people*—not numbers, but individuals.

If the church continues to adhere to God's view of sexuality and continues to declare that the only options for people with same-sex attractions are either celibacy or marriage to a member of the opposite sex, then the church must—this isn't optional—provide a safe and nurturing community for gay people to be a part of, especially people who remain celibate. We are to bear one another's burdens, not leave people to fend for themselves. So ask them what type of support they need. Invite them into your home to hear their story. Those with same-sex attractions don't necessarily need their own line of ministries; they need to feel welcomed into the ministries you already offer, without feeling awkward or unwanted. If individual ministries need to start, then do so, but first try to include people in the ministries currently running.

As I mentioned earlier, transformation happens within community. In light of transformation, we need to understand and teach the truth that our position in and acceptance by God is based on him and not on how well we behave (Ephesians 2:4-10). Christianity isn't about sin and behavior management but heart and life transformation, which come from Christ through the Holy Spirit. We can live self-controlled lives because of God's grace and power, not through trying harder and white-knuckling temptations (Titus 2:11-14). Again, we don't ignore sin and call evil things good, but neither do we hold up a standard of living for gay people that we don't follow ourselves.

Consider the impact on lives, if you joined together gay teens and young adults with Christlike men and women within the church. Educate and train people in being mentors whose main priority is to walk with others toward Jesus (we'll talk about this further in the next chapter). I praise God daily for the men who have walked beside me during my journey.[32] Their support, prayers, love, and God-honoring examples are invaluable treasures to me. The dominant "one another" verse in the New Testament is "love one another." As Christ loves us, so we love others. This is the simplicity of following Christ. Love LGBT people, and watch what God does through your relationships. Author and pastor Francis Chan writes these powerful words: "Pray that supernatural love begins to characterize our churches. Jesus said that the world would recognize us by our love and unity. Peter said that people would be compelled by our hope. But are *love, unity,* and *hope* the words that unbelievers use when describing your church?"[33] Are these the words gay people use to describe your church—their church?

ADAM SHARES

I met Adam a few months ago at a conference in South Carolina. He is the new executive director of OneByOne,[34] a ministry within the Presbyterian Church USA. Adam's testimony is another powerful story of God working in the life of a man dealing with same-sex attractions. Adam is a full-time seminary student, earning his master's of divinity. I asked him to share some thoughts about his experience as a teenager and young adult within the church. Adam said he didn't feel church was a safe place to open up about his sexuality and struggles. He didn't feel safe at youth group either, because many of the kids made homophobic remarks. Because of this, Adam stayed silent and struggled alone for years. He continues sharing:

> I didn't open up to anyone in the church about my same-sex attractions (SSA) until I met Bill Henson, executive director of Lead Them Home.[35] Bill was welcoming new people to a Celebrate Recovery meeting at Grace Chapel, my home church. For the very first time, here was someone sharing openly about their SSA and homosexual past to a group inside a church. This was groundbreaking for me, and the divine appointment I needed to finally reveal my deepest and most personal struggle. After Bill shared, he broke us up into small groups according to our struggles. I met with Bill and one other man who was struggling with a porn addiction. That night I told both guys about my SSA and all the pain I was dealing with. Apart from being attracted to men from a very early age, I shared the frustration of always feeling like an outsider whenever I was in a group of my peers, alienated by the world of sports and roughhousing. Bill empathized with me

and assured me that no matter what path I chose, he and his ministry would always be there with unconditional love and support. This made a deep impact on me. I continued to reach out to Bill as a mentor throughout my college years, and he was always there, just as he promised. After my fiancée and I got engaged, Bill invited us to a dinner hosted at his home. The company consisted of couples like us—a husband struggling with SSA. It was extremely helpful to hear their stories, and both my fiancée and I gleaned a tremendous amount of insights that night. We now have a group of couples, at different stages in their journeys, to go to as a resource.

CHURCH LEADER QUESTIONS TO DISCUSS

Below are some questions designed for you to work through as a leadership team. Don't just put down vague "church answers." Write out specific answers and steps. Search your heart and strive to discern what God is asking of your church.

- As a church, are we prepared to welcome those in the gay community? If not, why not? What are the fears and issues we need to start working through in order to do this?

- As a church, what is our position on homosexuality, and how will we talk about this—from the pulpit, in small groups, in youth ministry, in Sunday school, and in other settings?

- As a church, how will we balance truth and grace? What does this look like?

- When talking about sin, are we talking about all sin or just the "big ones"?

- What does our church discipline look like? How does this affect the people involved?

- How will we make sure that we as a church offer restoration and reaffirmation, including toward people who have gone through a church discipline process? [Check out 2 Corinthians 2–5 for a good place to start.]

- How does discipleship work in our church? What are we doing right? How can we improve?

- What does discipleship in our church look like for a person struggling with same-sex attractions? How are we plugging them into other ministries? Are we meeting their needs? If not, what do we need to change/add in order to do so?

- What types of training and resources do we need to look into?

- How will we handle gay people wanting to be leaders in the church?

- As a church, will we ever hire a pastor, youth pastor, worship leader, children's pastor, or staff member who struggles with same-sex attractions? If no, why not? What are our fears or concerns? Do we have a biblical reason for not hiring them?

- How can we prepare our church and families to accept hiring such a person?

- Are there families currently in our church who are dealing with homosexuality? How can we start helping them in this journey?

- Are there individuals currently in our church who have same-sex attractions? How can we start helping them in this journey?

- As a church, how will we start reaching out to the gay community around us? How are we praying for them? How are we praying for those within our fellowship who are gay?

CHAPTER 11:

BEING A MENTOR

The parable of the prodigal son leaves us hanging. In fact, many of the stories we read in the Gospels leave us wondering, "What happened next?" Here's an answer I'd like to suggest: Because the parables were for those listening to Jesus (as well as for us), and they were meant to change the mindsets and lives of the hearers, then maybe Jesus is waiting for us to finish the story. Maybe the parable endings are what we make of them. Jesus has told us what to do; now it's up to us to live out what he's taught. By allowing the Spirit to change us, we allow God to use us in bringing change to the world around us.

I've tried to make this book practical for church leaders and families. I am simply adding my voice and experiences to the overall conversation. My challenge to you is to take what you've learned and considered here, and put into action the things God has revealed to you. Don't let God's call and challenge to you die here. Though it may be intimidating and overwhelming, know that God has a purpose for you reading this book (and others on this topic). God doesn't give us information simply to have knowledge. In everything, there's a divine purpose. Answer the call God is giving your ministry, your church, and your family.

One way you can answer that call is to pursue a path of mentoring.

COUNSELING AS MENTORING

Youth workers frequently ask me, *"How do you mentor someone who's gay?"* This is a great question, and, for me, one with an easy answer. Most of us understand the strategy of mentoring other teenagers through Bible studies, praying together, life-on-life interaction, and other helpful disciplines. Well, mentor gay teens the same way. If the teenager doesn't know Jesus, then this is where you begin. If the teenager knows Jesus but has questions and doubts—which all teens do—start there. Ministry to gay teens is about building relationships, investing time into their lives, and challenging them to see Christ for who he really is and to see themselves in the same manner. It's about walking alongside students regardless of the outcome, and trusting Jesus every step of the way, because he is sovereign.

Remember, you're not meeting with them to solve the issue of them being gay. You're there to help gay teens get and stay grounded in Jesus. When I meet with teenagers and adults, I make sure they know (especially parents) that I am not a licensed counselor, so the only "counseling" I do is pastoral. I'm not there to make them or their child straight; I'm there to help them connect with and follow Jesus. In my ministry, the bottom goal is focusing on God's identity and wholeness for people through spiritual formation and discipleship.[36]

When meeting a new person, I start by listening to their story: *Tell me about yourself. What's going on? Tell me about your same-sex attractions. What's life at home like? Are you out to your parents or friends, and if not, why not?* After listening to them, I ask how I can help them in this journey. Usually, their answer is that they want me to help them not be gay anymore. Most have read my testimony and figure that because I'm married and have kids, I can help them achieve the same goal. This is where I need to be real with people and give honest hope. I let teens and adults know where I am with things: Though I'm married and very attracted to my wife, she is the only woman I am attracted to, and there are occasions when my same-sex attractions emerge as temptations.

I ask them what their definition of change looks like, and then I explain to them my definition. Change, for me, means that I'm becoming more like Christ and less like myself, whether my same-sex attractions go away or not. I try to explain that same-sex attractions don't define us, our future, or our walk with Christ. They're a part of us and make us unique, but they don't discredit us from seeking and serving Jesus. I let people know that I've friends who once dealt with same-sex attractions but no longer do so—they consider themselves totally straight, and they're happily married now. I also share with them that I've other friends who have stories resembling mine, while other friends have chosen to live celibate lives because they have no desire to marry the opposite sex. I assure them that Jesus acknowledges all three examples, none of which makes them more or less of a man (or woman).

Most often, in my experience with people, porn activity and addiction come up in the conversation, especially the use of gay porn. I let people know that this could definitely fuel their same-sex attractions. They're training their minds to get aroused by the images they're viewing, and the longer they view such stimulation, the more intense their attractions will become. I ask about the type of boundaries they have in place to help with their porn use, and I give them some boundaries that helped with my addiction.

This would be an appropriate time to ask teenagers if they're experimenting sexually. If they are, advise them to stop—just as you would if a straight teenager came to you and said they were having sex. Point out some realistic dangers of sex, especially if they're having unprotected sex. If the teen isn't sexually active, advise them to stay this way—again, pointing out the consequences of being sexually intimate.

I do mention to teenagers that everything said during our times together is confidential, unless they pose a threat to themselves or others. Regarding sexual activity and porn use, I suggest they tell their parents what's going on. I offer to go with them for support or to tell the parents myself. But I do let the teenager know exactly what I'll be doing and saying, so as not to lose their trust in me. Obviously, this causes us to deal with them coming out to their parents if they haven't already done so. For help in this area, refer back to Chapter 3.

TURN THEIR FOCUS TO JESUS

After getting an understanding of where they are, I ask about their relationship with God: *What type of relationship do you have with God? What questions or doubts you have? Do you attend church, and are you part of a youth ministry?* As we've talked about in earlier chapters, most teenagers with a same-sex attraction have a hard time connecting to God. They believe they can't have one with the other. I encourage the teens I work with to keep pursuing God regardless, and to trust him along the way. God isn't threatened, put off, or even surprised by their same-sex attractions; he's a big God and can handle anything we bring to him.

Around this time, I ask them if they want to keep meeting and how often. I also discuss this with their parents, too. In choosing a place, I always prefer to meet in public areas, though in spots where our conversation can be private. You will want to help the teenager feel comfortable and safe. On occasions, I will meet in my office at church, but only after I've received permission from the parent. Before we begin our meeting time, and before we end, I pray with the teenager—inviting them to pray, too, if they feel comfortable. Prayer is huge, and without it, this journey becomes impossible.

During our meeting times, I walk through what it means to follow Jesus. I usually start with the exercise I discussed in Chapter 5, concerning Romans 8. I want to hear their thoughts on who they think they are in Christ and how they see themselves generally. I focus on identity in the beginning because it's a vital core issue, as we discussed in Chapter 4. Depending on where the teenager wants to go from there, I also go through other books besides the Bible.[37] From this point, I strive to follow the Spirit's leading as I listen, pray, and share God's truth.

I'm not foolish to think this works for everybody—I know it doesn't. However, this is the main method I've used throughout the past five years of ministry, and in my experience, more people have pressed onward than have given up. Each person will require some different approaches, and some will progress further than others will. The important part is that you follow God's leading over your own, and that you rely on his strength over your own. Continually remember the words of Christ: *Apart from me, you can do nothing (John 15:5).* When ministering to gay teenagers, everything rides on this important truth.

A WORD ABOUT SIX:11 MINISTRIES

The purpose of our ministry is simple: to proclaim God's identity and wholeness. Grounded in biblical truth, Six:11 Ministries has a deep passion to reconnect people to their God-given identity, and to help them find fulfilling and lasting wholeness with God. We have a particular burden to challenge and disciple churches and people with same-sex attractions to center on Jesus together.

Started in 2007, Six:11 Ministries is a part of the Hope for Wholeness Network. More information about both ministries can be found online at six11.wordpress.com. Below are a few options we offer through our ministry to youth workers, church leaders, parents, and individuals.

ONLINE SUPPORT

The main outlet of our ministry is online. Through our blog, we strive to present effective resources, discussion, and insight about topics for the global church. While we do vary our conversations, the main topic of this blog is homosexuality. The blog offers specific resources for youth workers and parents, along with a recommended "bookshelf."

PASTORAL COUNSELING

Shawn is a licensed pastor with the Christian & Missionary Alliance church. He offers pastoral counseling to students and adults, centering on spiritual formation and discipleship. He doesn't diagnose and treat people. Student counseling is only done with parent *and* student permission. Counseling can be done via email, phone, or face to face. All counseling is free.

TEACHING AND CONSULTING

Since 2007, Shawn has had the opportunity to teach at churches, colleges, and conferences on topics such as sexuality, homosexuality, teen culture, evangelism, and our identity in Christ. He is also a consultant for churches and student ministries on how to meet the needs of the world around them, including those in the LGBT community. To schedule Shawn to come speak, please visit six11.wordpress.com.

ENDNOTES

Chapter 1

[1] In this book, I use gay to speak generally of the gay, lesbian, and bisexual community. While each group is different in its own specifics, I speak in generality because at the core of this conversation, how one responds and ministers to them is the same. This book doesn't address the complexity and uniqueness of transgender teens, unless noted otherwise. However, it's my conviction that the same advice given here can generally apply to transgender teens. I also use the word *gay* and the phrase *someone who has/struggles with same-sex attractions* interchangeably. Both mean the same thing because both describe a part of who the individual is. It shouldn't be assumed that referring to one as gay means the person is sexually active or that the person doesn't hold to a traditional view of Scripture. When a difference is being made, I make such a reference.

[2] npr.org/templates/story/story.php?storyId=183189088

[3] health.usnews.com/health-news/news/articles/2013/05/16/anti-gay-bullying-tied-to-teen-depression-suicide

Chapter 2

[4] This isn't his real name.

[5] Gay Christian Network (GCN) interviewed about 3,000 evangelical students concerning homosexuality. When asked to respond to the statement "People have control over whether they're gay or straight," 63.5 percent either agreed or strongly agreed. When

presented with the statement "Some people are born gay," 65.7 percent either disagreed or strongly disagreed. The survey can be accessed here: gaychristian.net/pr/gcn-college-survey-111113.php.

[6] A.W. Tozer, *The Knowledge of the Holy* (New York, NY: HarperCollins, 1961), 103.

[7] singleparents.about.com/od/legalissues/p/portrait.htm

[8] Joe Dallas spoke during the Hope for Wholeness Conference in October 2013, in Greenville, South Carolina.

[9] gaychristian.net/pr/gcn-college-survey-111113.php

[10] Darrin Patrick, *Church Planter* (Wheaton, IL: Crossway, 2010), 175.

Chapter 3

[11] Mike Yaconelli, *The Core Realities of Youth Ministry* (Grand Rapids, MI: Zondervan, 2003), 117.

[12] Check out our blog for recommended books and resources: six11.wordpress.com/resources/book-shelf/.

[13] I highly recommend the resources of xxxchurch.com and covenanteyes.com.

[14] Tim Geiger, "Providing Comfort and Hope to Hurting Parents." This article begins on page 81 of the book *The Homosexual Debate and the Church: A Collection of Essays* published by Harvest USA in 2006.

[15] Ibid., 81.

[16] Ibid., 85.

Chapter 4

[17] For more information about Chris and his powerful work in the area of our identity in Christ, visit chrismcalister.com.

[18] A sample of this covenant can be found on my blog, six11.wordpress.com/youth-workers.

Chapter 5

[19] Patrick, *Church Planter,* 137.

[20] bibleapps.com/greek/1377.htm

[21] studylight.org/lex/grk/gwview.cgi?n=5381

[22] A.W. Tozer, *The Knowledge of the Holy* (New York, NY: HarperCollins, 1961), 1.

[23] Chris McAlister, *SightShift: Identity* (Columbus, OH: SightShift Publishing, 2013), 40-41.

[24] Neil T. Anderson, *Victory Over the Darkness* (Ventura, CA: Regal Books, 2000), 47.

[25] McAlister, *SightShift: Identity,* 136-138.

Chapter 6

[26] Find more answers and resources for churches and families at six11.wordpress.com/youth-workers.

[27] Taken from glaad.org/transgender/trans101.

Chapter 7

[28] Mike Haley, *101 Frequently Asked Questions About Homosexuality* (Eugene, OR: Harvest House Publishers, 2004), 42.

[29] For more information about the Hope For Wholeness network, visit hopeforwholeness.org.

Chapter 9

[30] Two books I highly recommend are *101 Frequently Asked Questions About Homosexuality* by Mike Haley, and *When Homosexuality Hits Home* by Joe Dallas.

Chapter 10

[31] Thom and Joani Schultz, *Why Nobody Wants to Go to Church Anymore* (Loveland, CO; Group Publishing, 2013), 94.

[32] There are way too many people to name, and I'm sure I will forget someone, but I do want to acknowledge Pete, Tom, Doug, Rich, Craig, Barney, Mikey, Pat, Bob L., Bob S., Darrin, and my dad.

[33] Francis Chan, *Multiply* (Colorado Springs, CO; David C. Cook, 2012), 72.

[34] oneby1.org

[35] leadthemhome.org

Chapter 11

[36] For more information about Six:11 Ministries, visit six11.wordpress.com/about/.

[37] Check out our blog for recommended books and resources: six11.wordpress.com/resources/book-shelf/.

NOTES

NOTES

MINISTERING TO GAY TEENAGERS